UNRAVELLING CAP[ITAL]
A Guide to Marxist Pol[itical Economy]

Joseph Choonara

C000314615

UNRAVELLING CAPITALISM

A Guide to Marxist Political Economy

Joseph Choonara

bookmarks publications

Unravelling Capitalism: A Guide to Marxist Political Economy
Joseph Choonara

First published in May 2009 by Bookmarks Publications
c/o 1 Bloomsbury Street, London WC1B 3QE
© Bookmarks Publications

Cover image No.022 Archimedes' Dream by Makoto Tojiki Design
Typeset by Bookmarks Publications
Printed by Aldgate Press

ISBN 978 1905 192 502

Contents

Introduction 7

Part 1: Understanding the system
A system that hides its secrets 12
Marx's value 19
Money makes the world go round 26
Living and dead labour 29
Exploitation at the heart of the system 33
The anatomy of capital 36
Squeezing the worker 41
Productive and unproductive labour 45
The reserve army of labour 49
A world of alienation 52

Part 2: Dynamics of the system
The circulation of capital 58
Capital's self-expansion 66
Accumulate, accumulate! 68
The falling rate of profit 74
Counteracting influences 79
Capitalism and crisis 84
An ageing system 90
The distribution of surplus value 95
The world of finance 97
Fictitious capital 104
A second look at crisis 107
Prices and the general rate of profit 113
Politics of the crisis 119

Part 3: The changing system
The classical period 124
The birth of imperialism 128
The slump and state capitalism 131
The long boom 134
The return of crisis 138

Appendix 1: Marx's theory of rent 147
Appendix 2: The "transformation problem" 151

Further reading 154
Index 158

Introduction

THE failures of capitalism have provoked a growing interest in Marxist political economy. The aim of this work is to address that interest, introducing Marx's ideas and showing, at least in outline, how they can be applied to the capitalist system today.

As I write, at the end of 2008, the failures of capitalism are greatly in evidence. The collapse of the US housing bubble in autumn 2007 triggered a financial panic which is now becoming a new global slowdown. According to the International Monetary Fund we are already in the midst of the "largest financial shock since the Great Depression" of the 1930s. Nobody knows how deep the problems are or how long they will last, but three things are clear. First, a series of bubbles in the world economy masked what from a Marxist perspective has been apparent for many years: the poor health of the "real" economy compared to the sustained period of growth during the 1950s and 1960s. Second, those at the commanding heights of the US Federal Reserve, the British Treasury, and the boardrooms of banks and multinationals have no coherent theory of their own system. They swing from wild panic to glib optimism. Third, politics is, as Lenin wrote, "concentrated economics". Crisis exacerbates all the political divisions within the system.

Splits and infighting erupt both within the ruling class over how to solve the crisis and between different national ruling classes as they seek to shift the burden of the crisis onto each other, intensifying imperialist conflict. Simultaneously every ruling class seeks to make its own working class pay for the crisis.

The recent acute failures of capitalism are compounding its longer term chronic failures. This is expressed most sharply by the fate of those in the poorer countries, now all drawn firmly into the capitalist sphere. According to the United Nations, about one billion people currently live on the equivalent of less than $1 a day; 2.6 billion, 40 percent of the world's population, live on less than $2 a day. Behind these dry statistics stand untold suffering and misery, matched only by the heroic resistance of workers in countries such as Egypt or Bolivia in recent years.

The horror of life for the majority in what is known as the Third World finds an echo even in the wealthiest parts of the system. In the US, the richest economy the world has ever seen, a fifth of all children are brought up in poverty (defined as families with less than half the median income). Workers suffer increased stress and long hours—for manufacturing workers the working year has increased by two weeks over the past couple of decades. Meanwhile a tiny minority have accumulated riches on a scale never seen before. The richest 1 percent in the US now receive over 20 percent of total income, twice their share in the 1970s. The sharp division between rich and poor is echoed in every society. The Third World boasts its own contingent of the super-rich, who form part of a global capitalist elite. Overall the richest one hundred millionth of the world's population own as much as the poorest half of the world's population.

It was in the context of capitalism's failure that a new period of resistance began in the late 1990s. The growing anti-capitalist sentiment became most visible in 1999 on the streets of Seattle, where protesters shut down the

World Trade Organisation meeting in the city, and outside the 2001 G8 summit in the Italian city of Genoa. But the movement on the streets was a reflection of far wider distrust of the multinationals and the power of those supposedly governing the capitalist system. For many of those involved in the anti-capitalist movement their initial concerns were economic inequality and the plunder of the Third World. Recently many have gone on to protest against the cycle of wars initiated by the US's rulers after 11 September 2001. Some are involved in debates over global warming and the threat to humanity this poses.

Each of these issues is tied to a much wider concern—to explain the workings and malfunctionings of the capitalist system, to understand its strengths and its vulnerabilities and ultimately to seek its overthrow. Marxism is not a recipe book that can magically solve any of these problems. But it is an indispensable set of tools at the service of a movement with these aims. The growing interest in Marxist economics is not misplaced.

Thanks to Chris Harman, Alex Callinicos, Mark Thomas and Jennifer Braunlich. I owe them each a debt for encouraging me to write this book, and for their corrections and suggestions at various stages of its production.

Unravelling Capitalism

Part 1

UNDERSTANDING THE SYSTEM

A system that hides its secrets

IN 1872 Karl Marx dashed off a letter applauding plans to publish a French edition of the first volume of *Capital* in serial form. "In this form the book will be more accessible to the working class, a consideration that outweighs everything else," Marx wrote.

Capital is rather different from traditional treatises on economics. There are passages that drip with venom:

> Within the capitalist system, all methods for raising the social productiveness of labour are brought about at the cost of the individual labourer. They mutilate the labourer into a fragment of a man, degrade him to the level of an appendage of a machine, destroy every remnant of charm in his work and turn it into hated toil.

The three volumes of *Capital* produced by Marx were written with a single purpose: to grasp capitalism's "laws of motion" in order to hasten its overthrow. The main audience was the group in society that Marx saw as key to overthrowing capitalism—the emerging working class. But he feared that readers might be "disheartened" by their attempts to grapple with *Capital*. "There is no royal road to science, and only those who do not dread the fatiguing climb of its steep paths have a chance of gaining its luminous summits," Marx concluded in his letter to his French publisher. The difficulty many readers face is not primarily due to Marx's writing style but to his subject matter—capitalism.

Capitalism is a particular "mode of production". Since humans emerged as a species, they have discovered different ways to work together to produce the things they need, different modes of production. At Marx's funeral his close friend and collaborator, Frederick Engels, explained how Marx made this the basis for a wider understanding of how particular societies worked:

> Just as Darwin discovered the law of development of organic nature, so Marx discovered the law of development of human history: the simple fact, hitherto concealed by an overgrowth of ideology, that mankind must first of all eat, drink, have shelter and clothing, before it can pursue politics, science, art, religion, etc; that therefore the production of the immediate material means, and consequently the degree of economic development attained by a given people or during a given epoch, form the foundation upon which the state institutions, the legal conceptions, art, and even the ideas on religion, of the people concerned have been evolved, and in the light of which they must, therefore, be explained, instead of vice versa, as had hitherto been the case.

Economics ought not to be a dry academic discipline explaining just one facet of our life in isolation. It is fundamental to what makes us human, describing how we meet our immediate needs, which in turn makes everything else that takes place in society possible. The particular way in which humans produce has varied enormously. Centuries ago our ancestors might have hunted, gathered edible plants or farmed. Today we harness great concentrations of advanced machinery to produce everything from food and clothing to televisions and fridges.

Perhaps the most striking difference between capitalism and what came before it is what happens to the things that are produced. In earlier societies people worked mainly to produce goods for their own consumption, but capitalism is different. The workers in a car plant cannot eat cars and forego food; the staff in a McDonald's restaurant cannot build houses or cars out of burgers. The goods produced under capitalism are not produced to meet immediate needs; they are produced to sell. As Marx writes on the first page of *Capital*, "The wealth of those societies in which the capitalist mode of production prevails presents itself as an immense accumulation of commodities."

Capitalism is a system of commodity production. Goods are produced for the market. But this very fact can conceal the workings of the system and disguise its "laws of motion". Consider a simple economic act under capitalism such as purchasing a newspaper at a corner shop. Money leaves your hands and in return you get a commodity. On the surface this looks like a relationship between things—a newspaper for some coins. But it raises an important question: where did the newspaper come from? Journalists, editors, photographers and designers produced its contents. The words were reproduced by print workers, set in ink on paper that was the result of its own process of production, ultimately deriving from wood felled by a logger in some distant forest. The printing press and the journalists' computers were produced by yet more groups of workers. What seems at first to be a simple exchange of "things" in fact unlocks an endless network of relationships between people and, in particular, between groups of workers who produce commodities.

In earlier societies the relationships between people who produced goods were obvious. In capitalism they become hidden and mysterious. As Marx puts it, "a definite social relation between men" instead takes on "the fantastic form of a relationship between things". Marx calls this phenomenon the "fetishism of commodities". A "fetish" originally meant an object that was worshipped because people believed it contained a spirit or held some other mystical power. In capitalism things that are produced by humans seem to take on a life of their own—they become fetishised. There is a difference between this kind of fetishism and the mystical version. Under capitalism the powers that commodities seem to have are, in an important sense, real powers. Take, for example, money, a special "universal" commodity that can be exchanged for all others. The power of money is not like the power of a supernatural spirit that might frighten or awe people. Money *is* a source of real power. As Marx writes:

> The extent of the power of money is the extent of my power. Money's properties are my, the possessor's, properties and essential powers. Thus, what I *am and am capable of* is by no means determined by my individuality. I am ugly, but I can buy for myself the *most beautiful* of women. Therefore I am not ugly, for the effect of ugliness, its deterrent power, is nullified by money. I, according to my individual characteristics, am lame, but money furnishes me with 24 feet. Therefore I am not lame. I am bad, dishonest, unscrupulous, stupid; but money is honoured, and hence its possessor. Money is the supreme good, therefore its possessor is good. Money, besides, saves me the trouble of being dishonest: I am therefore presumed honest. I am *brainless*, but money is the *real brain* of all things and how then should its possessor be brainless? Besides, he can buy clever people for himself, and

is he who has a power over the clever not more clever than the clever? Do not I, who thanks to money am capable of *all* that the human heart longs for, possess all human capacities? Does not my money, therefore, transform all my incapacities into their contrary?

Money even seems to attract more money, for instance through interest payments or through the ability of the super-rich to invest in hedge funds or gamble on stock markets. Money has real power, but the *reason why* money has these powers, the social root of its power, is mystified. The same is true of commodities in general.

Marx's writings, especially *Capital*, are complex because he sought to penetrate the surface appearance of capitalism and examine the social relationships between humans. Only these relationships can explain how the system works or indeed why it goes wrong.

At first glance capitalism seems hopelessly complicated. Phenomena such as inflation, the workings of derivatives and futures markets, or the nature of "structured investment vehicles" and "collateralised debt obligations" are perplexing for anyone encountering them for the first time. Faced with this, there are two temptations. The first is to explain these manifestations in their own terms: to accept the mystified surface appearance of capitalism. If stock markets and hedge funds seem to magically generate value out of thin air, some economists argue, this is what must happen. The second temptation is to simplify things down to the most basic level and ignore the more complicated aspects of the system.

Marx's method avoids both traps. He starts by recognising the mystified surface appearance: "All science would be superfluous if the outward appearance and the essence of things directly coincided." To discover the "laws of motion" of capitalism a scientific approach is needed. For Marx that means it is necessary to *abstract* from the misleading appearance of things.

Here Marx's approach is analogous to that taken by the great scientist Isaac Newton when he discovered his own famous laws of motion. These too were the product of abstraction. Newton's first law of motion states that objects will move in a straight line at a constant speed until a force acts upon them. But a brick sitting on the Earth's surface, when moved, will quickly grind to a halt. Newton had to ask what would happen if the effects of friction and air resistance were removed. This is an example of an abstraction. Strip out the surface features that confuse the picture and consider its most basic elements.

But abstraction is only half of the scientific method. Newton's laws of motion have to explain not just abstract laws but also the way the world actually appears, the world in which bricks grind to a halt rather than continuing in straight lines at a constant speed. This means integrating the abstract laws of motion together with those of friction and air resistance to explain the actual motion of things. Similarly, Marx seeks to understand the most basic processes in capitalism *and* then to reconstruct ever more complex aspects of the system in his theory. Once this is done it becomes clear how the basic "laws of motion" generate the complicated surface appearance. As Marx writes in the *Grundrisse*, a draft of *Capital* in which he worked out many of his ideas, we arrive back where we started, but "this time not as the chaotic conception of a whole, but as a rich totality of many determinations and relations".

Needless to say, this process is open ended. Not only does capitalism contain many phenomena that are difficult to grasp; it also changes as it ages and develops.

Theory can never keep pace with the changing world. This is one of the reasons why Marx notoriously found it difficult to actually complete any of his major works. *Capital* is no exception. Initially several volumes were planned. Only the first was published in Marx's lifetime. The second and third volumes were drawn together by Frederick Engels from unfinished manuscripts and published posthumously. It is in these often difficult pages that we can find the outlines of a revolutionary new understanding of capitalism.

Marx's value

CAPITAL begins with a simple question: what makes one commodity exchange for another? Why might a pint of milk cost the same as a copy of a newspaper? These two commodities have different uses and qualities. They are produced in different ways. So why are they worth the same amount of money? What is the connection between the two?

Marx argues that all commodities have two kinds of value. The first is simply its usefulness, or use-value. "The utility of a thing makes it a use-value," writes Marx. "But this utility is not a thing of air. Being limited by the physical properties of the commodity, it has no existence apart from that commodity." In other words, the thing that our two commodities have in common is definitely not their use-value. They have very different physical properties and very different uses. It is not possible to read milk or drink a newspaper.

The second kind of value is exchange-value, which is the amount of one commodity that you can get for another. In our example, one newspaper might exchange for one pint of milk so they have the same exchange-value. Exchange-value is not a reflection of use-value. The air we breathe is of enormous use to us because we would die without it but it has no exchange-value. The B-2 stealth bomber might have very limited use-value as far as most people are concerned but it has a very high exchange-value—it is worth about 500 million pints of milk.

So, where does exchange-value come from? We already know that when I go into a shop and exchange money for a commodity such as a newspaper or a pint of milk I am tapping into a vast network of social relationships that went into producing these commodities. Marx points out that all commodities have a certain important property in common: they are the product of a certain quantity of human labour. He argues that beneath the surface of exchange-value lies something else, a thing that he calls simply "value".

The value of a commodity reflects the amount of labour that went into producing it. This value can be measured: "The quantity of labour…is measured by its duration…in weeks, days and hours."

But what exactly is value? To return to an analogy we used in the previous chapter, here value is an abstraction that plays a role a bit like gravity does in Isaac Newton's picture of the universe. We cannot see, touch or smell gravity. However, the concept allows us to understand why the planets go round the sun. The effects of gravity are real, as anyone falling down a mineshaft realises. Of course, there is a difference. Value is a product of human society, while gravity would exist regardless. But in a capitalist society value *appears* as an eternal, natural law shaping the world independent of our will, even though it is in reality bound up with a particular period of history.

So, in a capitalist society at least, value allows us to understand why two commodities have the same exchange-value. We cannot directly observe value but its effects are real. Capitalism is a system for drawing values together, equating them and exchanging them. Value is the one thing that can do this because it reflects the one property that all commodities have in common—the human labour that goes into producing them. Already

Marx has made a radical point. Commodities do not acquire their value because of the genius of the entrepreneur or the machinery brought together by the capitalist in the factory; commodities have value because workers create them.

To understand why value can play such a crucial role under capitalism it is necessary to consider one additional and well known feature of the system—competition. As we shall see, it is competition that actually enforces the law of value, for instance by forcing capitalists to behave as capitalists, however well intentioned they might otherwise be. Marx is sometimes accused of ignoring the "laws of supply and demand", which, in mainstream accounts of competition, are used to explain changes in prices. In fact Marx recognised the importance of supply and demand, but realised that they could not account for value on their own. In a speech in 1865 he explained:

> You would be altogether mistaken in fancying that the value of...any...commodity whatever is ultimately fixed by supply and demand. Supply and demand regulate nothing but the temporary *fluctuations* of market prices. They will explain to you why the market price of a commodity rises above or sinks below its *value*, but they can never account for the *value* itself. Suppose supply and demand to equilibrate, or, as the economists call it, to cover each other. Why, the very moment these opposite forces become equal they paralyse each other, and cease to work in the one or other direction. At the moment when supply and demand equilibrate each other, and therefore cease to act, the *market price* of a commodity coincides with its *real value*, with the standard price round which its market prices oscillate.

Supply and demand make market prices oscillate around value. They prevent these prices from deviating too far from value, but they do not *explain* value. Indeed, one of Marx's main criticisms of existing economic theory was its failure to explain the origin of value. Adam Smith and later David Ricardo, the two greatest figures in classical political economy who preceded Marx, came closest. For instance, Smith believed that in early societies, where the barter of goods directly produced by individuals predominated, exchange was explained by a labour theory of value. "Labour", wrote Smith, "is the real measure of the exchangeable value of all commodities." But, rather than follow the theory to its logical conclusion, Smith retreated into a view that saw machinery as generating "revenue" alongside labour. Ricardo came even closer to Marx's position, but never developed his labour theory of value into a consistent approach that could explain the dynamics of the system.

Later mainstream economists stepped back from trying to explain capitalism as a system at all. By Marx's lifetime capitalism had established itself as the dominant system of production in key areas of the globe. Its theoreticians were now far more interested in superficial fluctuations in prices and in covering up the crimes of the system than in discovering its fundamental laws of motion. This was reflected in a shift from the term "political economy", concerned with social and historical development of the system, to "economics" concerned with seemingly eternal mathematical laws of the market. It was left to Marx to build on and criticise Smith and Ricardo's political economy in order to develop a systematic labour theory of value.

There is, however, an obvious objection to Marx's theory: not everyone's labour is the same. Some people work harder or more efficiently than others. As Marx writes, "Some people might think that if the value of a commodity is determined by the quantity of labour spent on it, the more idle and unskilful the labourer, the more valuable would his commodity be, because more time would be required in its production." This problem is overcome if you consider "socially necessary labour time": the labour time needed by a society to produce a commodity with the "average degree of skill and intensity prevalent at the time". This is the kind of labour that capitalism draws together. It creates a world in which all artistry is removed from work by the application of machinery and the division of labour. It simultaneously creates a world of millions of "interchangeable" workers, each, from the point of view of the capitalist, the same as the others. Indeed, the fact that capitalism is a system of competition forces capitalists to treat labour in this way—failure to do so would mean the capitalists in question losing out to their rivals.

Of course, under capitalism some particular skills will be especially valuable and prized. One obvious example is the labour that goes into the production of expensive artworks. The value of a painting by Rembrandt clearly does not reflect the time he took to produce it. But then the labour of Rembrandt could never be reduced to socially necessary labour time because it is not labour that could be performed by anyone else; it could only have been performed by Rembrandt. What are prized in such artworks are the specific, concrete characteristics of the labour that went into producing it. The logic of capitalism is to subordinate everything to the market—so a Rembrandt painting is turned into a commodity to be bought and sold, but its price bears no relation to the labour time it contains. Similarly Marx writes that the poet Milton "produced *Paradise Lost* in the way that a silkworm produces silk, as the expression of *his own* nature", even if later "he sold the product for £5 and to that extent became a dealer in a commodity". Marx contrasts this with the "writer who delivers hackwork for his publisher". The "literary proletarian who produces books, eg compendia on political economy, at the instructions of his publisher" *is* subject to the laws of capitalist production, precisely because this kind of work could be performed by any of thousands of other wage labourers.

Marx is also aware that some "skilled labour" exists under capitalism. But this phrase can have two very different meanings. The first could be called "intense labour". If a worker, by virtue of some special training or ability, can produce twice as much of a good or service than the "average" worker in a given period of time, then they clearly create more value for the capitalist (and may attract a greater wage too). But a skilled worker can also mean a "specialised worker" whose training allows them to perform certain roles.

Here it should be understood that the level of skill and the precise combination of mental and physical exertion that a worker brings to bear on their work vary throughout history.

Abilities that many or even most workers have today—literacy and numeracy, the ability to drive a vehicle or use a computer—would seem extremely skilful to a worker in Marx's day (just as the manual dexterity of a mill worker in Marx's day might impress many workers today). Capitalism does not want each worker to be identical or to be able to do every single job. From the point of view of the system it is a waste of money for all workers to have degrees in chemistry. But it does need a large number of interchangeable workers who *do* have degrees in chemistry so that it can subordinate laboratory work to the laws of value.

Certain skills may start out as a monopoly among a tiny minority, and that tiny minority may, for a time, be strongly placed to force concessions such as better wages or conditions from the system. But over time capitalism tends to both reproduce workers with the skills it needs and, simultaneously, reduce skilled operations to less skilled ones. For example, if laboratory work previously carried out by chemists can instead be carried out by lab technicians without degrees, perhaps with the help of machinery and computers, then so much the better for the capitalist. The system constantly deskills the working class and refashions it, and breaks tasks apart and recombines them, ensuring that the overall tendency is the subordination of labour to the laws of capitalism.

Finally, Marx has been accused of failing to "prove" his labour theory of value. But this accusation is misplaced. Marx does not set out to prove the existence of value or to derive the market prices of particular commodities from first principles. His theory reflects what capitalism actually does: it draws socially necessary labour together at different points in the system and produces commodities that can be exchanged based on this labour. It is from this perspective that Marx could begin to explore the development of capitalism. The ultimate test of his labour theory of value is its ability to explain the dynamics of the system.

Money makes the world go round

RETURNING to our example from the previous chapter, while it is true that a pint of milk might have the same exchange-value as a newspaper, it is unlikely that a newsagent would be inclined to swap a newspaper for a pint of milk provided by one of their customers. Under capitalism a third commodity, money, plays the role of the "universal commodity" and in doing so makes the whole process of exchange even more mysterious. How does money come to play this important role?

As we have seen, value is not something that we can touch or see directly. No commodity is produced with its value stamped upon it. It is measured indirectly by exchanging it with another commodity in a particular ratio: "one pint of milk = one newspaper"; "one car = 10,000 bars of chocolate"; "one stealth bomber = 500 million pints of milk".

As commodities are exchanged, a particular type of commodity can become a "universal equivalent". This development pre-dates the emergence of capitalism. Trade existed in earlier societies, but only as a peripheral feature—a matter of communities exchanging a small portion of what they produced with other communities, or peasants taking whatever surplus food they were left with to market. The commodity that became a universal equivalent might reflect the type of society it emerged from. For example, in early communities that traded livestock, cattle could become a universal equivalent due to its importance and the frequency with which it was traded. But generally precious metals such as gold and silver were found to play this role most effectively. Such metals are of high value relative to their weight. In other words, they require a large amount of labour time to produce a given quantity. This means that a large amount of value can be transported easily. Such metals are also hardwearing and durable so they can act as a reliable store of value.

As capitalism developed it seized hold of existing forms of money and transformed them. This was necessary because under capitalism commodity exchange plays an essential role in satisfying even the most basic human needs. Eventually states began to issue paper money, first in the form of bills that could be exchanged for "commodity money" (eg, gold or silver) and then, later, in the form of "inconvertible" bills. Such forms of money have no intrinsic value (other than as pieces of paper) and depend on the authority of the state or central bank that issues them.

Once a particular commodity establishes itself as the "universal equivalent" it has extraordinary power. It represents a claim on "socially necessary labour time" in whatever form. A £10 note can buy commodities of any kind, up to the equivalent of £10 worth of labour time. The goal of the capitalist in production is not to gain more commodities but to sell these commodities to get money—preferably more money than they started out with. This allows the capitalist to buy what is needed to begin a new cycle of production.

Previous ruling classes might have been interested in hoarding money to enrich themselves like misers. For the capitalist, as we shall see, money must be harnessed as capital. Marx defines capital as value that is used to generate more value—to make a profit. In other words, capital is "self-expanding" value. This drive to advance value in order to get more back, the drive to make a profit, is one of the things that defines capitalism as a system:

> The restless never-ending process of profit-making alone is what [the capitalist] aims at. This boundless greed after riches, this passionate chase after exchange-value, is common to the capitalist and the miser; but while the miser is merely a capitalist gone mad, the capitalist is a rational miser. The never-ending augmentation of exchange-value, which the miser strives after by seeking to save his money from circulation, is attained by the more acute capitalist by constantly throwing it afresh into circulation.

To understand capitalism we will have to explore how it is that value can be turned into capital—into value that expands by generating profit. But first we must look at the two kinds of capital purchased by the capitalist to begin the production process.

Living and dead labour

EARLIER I set out Marx's concept of value. The value of a commodity reflects the amount of labour time required in its creation. However, commodities are not simply produced by people. To return to an example we used previously, a newspaper is not just the product of journalists and print workers; machinery, computers, ink and paper are also needed in its production. But these too are commodities and hence the product of earlier acts of labour. So in capitalist production two kinds of labour come together. The first is what Marx calls "living labour", the labour put in directly by workers adding to the value of a new commodity. The second is "dead labour", labour that was expended in the past and crystallised in the form of raw materials and machinery used in the production process, described by Marx as the "means of production".

The value of the dead labour is transferred to the end product when the means of production are used by living labour, so the resulting commodity has a value reflecting the total amount of labour, past and present, required in its production. Marx discusses the example of a spinner who uses cotton and a spindle, which suffers wear and tear in the process, to produce yarn:

> In determining the value of the yarn, or the labour time required for its production, all the special processes carried on at various times and in different places, which were necessary, first to produce the

cotton and the wasted portion of the spindle, and then with the cotton and spindle to spin the yarn, may together be looked on as different and successive phases of one and the same process… If a definite quantity of labour, say 30 days, is requisite to build a house, the total amount of labour incorporated in it is not altered by the fact that the work of the last day is done 29 days later than that of the first. Therefore the labour contained in the raw material and the instruments of labour can be treated just as if it were labour expended in an earlier stage of the spinning process, before the labour of actual spinning commenced.

However, as we shall see, the distinction is important because only living labour adds new value to the end product. Consider a newspaper that is produced by one hour of living labour (the labour of the print workers who work the presses) plus two hours worth of dead labour (the value of raw materials consumed) per issue. Here, for simplicity, I will ignore the cost of the machinery involved or any other groups of workers such as the journalists. The total value of each newspaper is three hours worth of labour time. I will assume that the capitalist succeeds in selling all the newspapers.

Each newspaper:

1 hour	2 hours
living labour	dead labour

So the capitalists receive a value equivalent to three hours of labour time for each newspaper they sell. But the capitalist has to pay for the raw materials that are used up in the production of the newspaper. They have to purchase ink and paper from other capitalists. So the newspaper-producing capitalist has to pay two hours worth of value to other capitalists for each newspaper printed. The newspaper-producing capitalist makes neither a profit nor a loss on the raw materials that go into the production process (although the ink-producing or paper-producing capitalist would naturally expect that they would make themselves a profit by producing and selling these). The value of this dead labour simply passes into the final product.

So how does the newspaper-producing capitalist make a profit? As things stand at the moment, they have sold each newspaper for three hours worth of labour time and paid out two hours worth for raw materials. One hour's worth of labour time remains—the living labour added by the print workers to each newspaper. But our capitalist has still not paid anything to these workers. If, as Marx says, everything exchanges for its value, what is the price of living labour? If the print workers took home as their wage the full value they create (one hour's worth per newspaper) the capitalist would be left with nothing. However, we know from our experience that capitalists tend to make hefty profits.

The solution to this problem is central to Marx's whole analysis. He rightly refers to it as "one of the best points" in *Capital*. The workers produce new value worth one hour of labour time. But the capitalist does not pay the workers for the value they produce. Instead of paying the workers for their labour, the capitalist pays the workers for their "labour power"—for their ability to do a day's work. The value of labour power, the wage, is simply the value required to reproduce the labour power, to provide the worker with food, clothing, shelter and other needs. In general this is far less value than the worker creates.

In our example, if we assume that each print worker puts in eight hours of work a day, it might take just four hours of labour time to produce enough value to cover their wage. The other four hours do not produce anything for the worker but they produce what Marx called "surplus value" for the capitalist—extra, unpaid for, value. This surplus value is the basis of profit.

The point deserves to be stressed. *The capitalist gets a day's labour but only pays for a day's labour power.* Of course, the whole process is hidden behind a wage packet. It is not at all clear to the worker when they are working for their wage and when they are working to generate profit for the capitalist. As Marx puts it, "The fact that half a day's labour is necessary to keep the labourer alive during 24 hours does not in any way prevent him from working a whole day."

I have considered the gap between the value created by the worker in a day and the amount they take home in pay each day. I could equally look at how much of the living labour that goes into each commodity is surplus value and how much contributes to the wage. In our example, as half of the day is spent producing surplus value, so half of the living labour embodied in each newspaper (30 minutes worth of value) is surplus value.

Each newspaper:

30 mins	30 mins	2 hours
living labour		dead labour
wage	s	

s = surplus value

The secret of surplus value is the secret of the capitalist system. The world around us is based on pumping surplus value out of one billion or so wage workers.

Exploitation at the heart of the system

IN earlier societies exploitation was a relatively straight-forward process. The peasants in medieval Europe might work a few hours on their own land and a few hours on the land of their lord. Or they might work all day on their own land but have to surrender a portion of their product to the lord. It was clear to everyone involved that exploitation was going on. The lord could exploit the peasant because he was the political ruler as well as the economic ruler. Exploitation relied openly on the use of violence, or at least the threat of it.

Under capitalism economics appears to be separate from politics. At times the organised violence of the state might be used against workers who resist exploitation—for instance the army might be mobilised to break a strike. But in normal times the worker labours for the capitalist through pure economic compulsion, rather than the use or threat of violence. Those who have not inherited great wealth take it for granted that they must get a job working for a capitalist to survive. How did this kind of world come about?

The medieval peasant might have owned a plot of land or had access to some common land. They might have possessed a few sheep or cattle, or a plough and some grain. Under capitalism the worker owns none of the means of production. The *only* thing they have to sell is their labour power—under capitalism labour power itself becomes a commodity. Workers are under no obligation to work; they are not slaves. So the workers are "free" in a legal sense but, as Marx argues, they are also "free" in a second sense—free of all of the things they would need to produce for themselves and so free to starve if they refuse to work for a capitalist.

Towards the end of the first volume of *Capital*, in one of the most accessible parts of the book, Marx writes of the "original accumulation" (usually translated as "primitive accumulation") that marked the dawn of capitalism. This involved driving peasants from the land in countries such as Britain, with common land enclosed and turned over to farmers who now used capitalist methods. Such changes provided an impetus to early capitalism, just as they are doing in some areas of the developing world today. More importantly, they created a class of "free labourers", who drifted into towns and cities, and were forced to find work in the emerging capitalist enterprises centred there.

This situation did not come about through a natural process of evolution. Marx writes that capitalism comes into the world "dripping from head to foot, from every pore, with blood and dirt".

Once founded, the capitalist system must base itself on the exploitation of labour. The level of exploitation might vary in different places and at different times. However, it is a misconception that workers in countries such as India or China are more exploited than those in countries such as the US or Britain. This is not necessarily the case. They probably have worse pay and conditions, and face greater repression and degradation than workers in the most developed industrial countries. But it is also possible that workers in the US or Britain generate more surplus value for every pound that they are paid in wages. One of the strengths of Marx's theory is to show to that exploitation is not simply an exceptional condition faced by some unfortunate groups of workers—rather it is a universal condition of capitalist production. It will exist everywhere capitalism nestles and it will continue until capitalism is overthrown. It is this that unites workers in Britain with those in India, or those in the US with those in China.

The level of the wage may also vary. Contrary to what is sometimes claimed, Marx did not believe in an "iron law of wages" that would see pay reduced to the basic minimum needed for survival. Wages are subject to the day to day pressure that workers can bring to bear on capitalists through their struggles, and they vary in accordance with changes in the labour market (for example, shortages of labour can drive wages up for a time). They also contain what Marx called a historical and moral element, based on what workers have wrested out of capitalists in the past and come to expect, and on the changing cost of producing the kinds of labour capitalism needs.

Under capitalism workers begin to organise, struggle and demand a greater share in the wealth they create. But whatever the variations, the workers must labour longer than the time taken to generate enough new value to reproduce their labour power. Without exploitation there is no profit. Without an end to capitalism there can be no end to exploitation.

The anatomy of capital

T HE capitalist does not think about production in the same way that Marx did. As far as the capitalist is concerned, the dead labour of machinery and raw materials is as much the basis of profit as the living labour put in by workers in exchange for a wage. This misconception is reflected in much of mainstream economic theory, which sees different kinds of capital as "factors of production" each generating a return on investment for their owner.

Capital is simply value put forward with a view to gaining surplus value. When considering the system from this angle Marx refers to capital as divided into "constant" and "variable" capital. Constant capital is value advanced by the capitalist to purchase plant, equipment and raw materials. During the process of production it does not "undergo any quantitative alteration of value"—hence its name. Variable capital is the value advanced by the capitalist to purchase labour power. This does "undergo an alteration of value" in the production process, because "it both reproduces the equivalent of its own value and also produces an excess, a surplus value... I therefore call it the variable part of capital, or, shortly, *variable capital*."

To return to our example of the capitalist producing newspapers, we know that each newspaper represents three hours of labour time: two hours of dead labour and one hour of living labour. To make things clearer we can express values in money terms, rather than in terms of labour time. Say, for example, that £1 represents the value created by one hour of labour time. Then each newspaper will be worth £3.

Let us look again at how the one hour or £1 of living labour in our example is divided into surplus value and the value of labour power. We now know that the variable capital advanced by the capitalist goes to cover the wages of the workers whose labour power they exploit. Say that each print worker works an eight-hour day and that the value of their daily wage, the variable capital advanced each day, is four hours of labour time (ie £4). This would mean that half of the new value created by living labour each day simply covers the wage of the worker for that day; the other half is surplus value which goes to the capitalist in the form of profit. Similarly, if we look at the individual newspaper, half of the new value created by living labour and embodied in it goes towards the workers' wages and half of it is surplus value.

So another way of breaking down the value of each newspapers is:

Value of each newspaper
= Two hours constant capital + half an hour of variable capital + half an hour of surplus value
= £2 constant capital + 50p variable capital + 50p surplus value
= £3

Each newspaper:

50p	50p	£2
v	s	constant capital

v = variable capital; s = surplus value

Note that this diagram is almost identical to the one in the chapter on living and dead labour (although this time I have expressed the quantities in terms of money rather than time).

The capitalists get £3 for each newspaper they sell but they pay out £2 in raw materials (constant capital) and £0.50p in wages (variable capital). This leaves £0.50p per newspaper in profits (surplus value).

There are other ways that we can look at the exploitation of workers. Imagine there are 100 workers. They each work an eight-hour day, of which four hours worth covers their wage. So the total amount of new value created in a day is £800 (800 hours with each worth £1). We also know that £2 of dead labour are consumed for every £1 of living labour. So, for the whole workforce:

Total value of day's output
= 1,600 hours of dead labour + 800 hours of living labour
= 1,600 hours of constant capital + 400 hours of variable capital
+ 400 hours of surplus value
= £1,600 constant capital + £400 variable capital
+ £400 surplus value
= £2,400

In this example the capitalist invests £2,000 each day (the constant capital paid for raw materials plus the variable capital paid in wages) and gets £400 in profit each day.

Up to this point I have concentrated on the kind of constant capital that is completely consumed during the production process—for instance the ink and paper used in printing. The examples would hold perfectly well for other forms of constant capital, such as the printing press, assuming that the press was also completely consumed in the process of producing the newspapers. Of course, though, this assumption is unrealistic. Work would be unthinkable without vast accumulations of machinery and computers, not to mention office blocks and factories, which are used day in and day out without being fully consumed.

Plant and equipment of this kind, when it is purchased in order to generate surplus value, is a particular kind of constant capital, which Marx called "fixed capital". He contrasted fixed with "circulating capital". The distinction Marx draws centres on the way that value circulates. Circulating capital passes its value into the end product during the production process and this value circulates with the commodity as it enters the market. Fixed capital remains physically within the sphere of production and its value only gradually circulates, bit by bit, as it is used up over many production cycles. A printing press that costs £100,000 with a lifespan of ten years would, all other things remaining equal, each year pass £10,000 of value into the newspapers produced using it. Once we see how fixed capital gives up its value gradually we can treat it in much the same way as paper and ink in our examples.

It is not just the raw materials consumed in production that are circulating capital—ink and paper in our example—but also the variable capital (the capital advanced to purchase labour power). So variable capital is always circulating capital; its value (together with the surplus value it creates) always circulates with its products, whereas constant capital may be fixed or circulating. Marx criticised the mainstream economists of his day who simply saw a division between fixed and circulating capital, ignoring the more fundamental division between variable capital (whose expansion can produce surplus value) and constant capital (which can never produce surplus value whether it is fixed or circulating).

Although the division between fixed and circulating capital is less fundamental than the division between variable and constant capital, the concept of fixed capital is a useful way to understand a number of problems faced by the capitalist. First, while circulating capital can be bought on a regular basis by the capitalist at the beginning of each cycle of production, fixed capital is characteristically bought once and then used over many cycles of production. A printing press represents a huge investment, which the capitalist must expect to last for several years or even decades. This requires the capitalist to save large amounts of money over the preceding period or, more likely, to raise the funds some other way (for example by borrowing from a bank). The process of buying capital, producing and selling commodities becomes a lot less smooth and regular than it initially seems.

Second, and related to this, what happens if the value of printing presses changes during the lifetime of the press? We shall see later that values, particularly those of fixed capital, are far from stable. Prices tend to fall over time. This makes investment in fixed capital a risky business for the capitalist.

Third, the dangers inherent in this kind of investment intensify the need for the capitalist to squeeze the value out of fixed capital as rapidly as possible—for instance running a night shift as well as a day shift or ensuring that a factory is run 365 days a year.

Squeezing the worker

WE have already seen how capitalism is founded on exploitation, which allows the capitalist to obtain surplus value. In order to increase their profits capitalists must maximise the amount of surplus value they squeeze out of their workers. Already contained within Marx's account of the extraction of surplus value is the idea of a struggle between capitalist and workers.

One obvious way in which capitalists can increase their profits is by getting workers to toil longer and harder. In other words, they can increase the "absolute" surplus value produced by workers. If the worker covers the value of their wage in four hours but works an eight-hour day, the capitalist obtains four hours of surplus value. But if the worker works a ten-hour day, the capitalist obtains six hours of surplus value. In *Capital* Marx charts the battle over the length of the working day in England, which led to a series of Factory Acts, which limited the working day for women and children to ten hours:

> The English Factory Acts…curb the passion of capital for a limitless draining of labour power, by forcibly limiting the working day by state regulations, made by a state that is ruled by capitalist and landlord. Apart from the working class movement that daily grew more threatening, the limiting of factory labour was dictated by the same necessity which spread guano [bird faeces] over the English fields. The same

blind eagerness for plunder that in the one case exhausted the soil, had, in the other, torn up by the roots the living force of the nation. Periodical epidemics speak on this point as clearly as the diminishing military standard in Germany and France.

In other words, the attempt by the factory owners to extend the working day faced resistance from workers *and* threatened the health of the labourer. While Marx praises the factory inspectors, who he quotes extensively, for revealing the plight of the working class, from the point of view of the capitalists limiting the working day was not a case of philanthropy. It was a necessity if they were to have a working class to exploit. In addition, the poor health of workers threatened the strength of the military, which relied on workers to fight. This was unacceptable to the more farsighted capitalists who saw military strength as a means of securing their interests abroad. Marx's reference to the "diminishing military standard in Germany and France" is backed up by statistics showing that the minimum height for admission into the army had been reduced and the number of soldiers rejected had grown as capitalism had taken off.

Despite the existence of legal limits beyond which the working day cannot be extended, the drive to increase the number of hours worked has been an important factor in contemporary capitalism over the past couple of decades. So in the US manufacturing workers put in a full two weeks more a year in 2002 than they did in 1982—a huge boost to profits in that country. Capitalists also remain keen to reduce the amount of "rest" time in the working day. One in five workers in Britain do not take a lunch break, and accounts of "toilet breaks" and "coffee breaks" being monitored are commonplace. One account of "lean working" in the US speaks of attempts to increase the number of seconds worked in a minute to 57—three seconds of rest each minute.

However, the limits to such attempts to increase the extraction of absolute surplus value meant that increases in what Marx called "relative" surplus value became more important as capitalism developed. Increasing absolute surplus value means increasing the overall length of the working day, while leaving the time required to cover the wage of the worker unchanged. Increasing relative surplus value means decreasing the time the worker needs to cover the cost of their wage, while leaving the overall length of the working day unchanged. So, if a worker previously worked an eight-hour day and covered the cost of their wage in four hours, the capitalist can make more if the worker instead covers the cost of their wage in two hours.

Increasing absolute surplus value

1	2	3	4	5	6	7	8
	v				s		

v = 4 hours; s = 4 hours

1	2	3	4	5	6	7	8	9	10
	v					s			

v = 4 hours; s = 6 hours

Increasing relative surplus value

1	2	3	4	5	6	7	8
	v				s		

v = 4 hours; s = 4 hours

1	2	3	4	5	6	7	8
v				s			

v = 2 hours; s = 6 hours

v = variable capital; s = surplus value

One way the capitalist might achieve this is by arbitrarily cutting wages. But, as in the case of extending the working day, there are clearly limits to this: resistance and the possibility that workers will be too sick or underfed to work. However, an increase in relative surplus value can occur gradually if the value of the goods and services workers purchase with their wage falls. For instance, if food and clothing become cheaper, in terms of the amount of labour time that goes into producing them, then the share of the value going to the worker can fall without the worker having to consume fewer use-values. We will see later that technological change can indeed cheapen commodities of all kinds.

Productive and unproductive labour

CAPITALIST production creates use-values but when capitalists purchase constant and variable capital they do so primarily in order to generate surplus value, the source of profit. Under capitalism all sorts of work also takes place that does not directly generate surplus value, and the scale of this kind of work has expanded as capitalism has developed. To understand such work Marx begins by making a distinction between what he calls "productive" and "unproductive" labour. He writes:

> Capitalist production is not merely the production of commodities, it is essentially the production of surplus value. The labourer produces not for himself, but for capital. It no longer suffices, therefore, that he should simply produce. He must produce surplus value. That labourer alone is productive who produces surplus value for the capitalist and thus works for the self-expansion of capital... The notion of a productive labourer implies not merely a relation between work and useful effect, between labourer and product of labour, but also a specific, social relation of production, a relation that has sprung up historically and stamps the labourer as the direct means of creating surplus value. To be a productive labourer is, therefore, not a piece of luck, but a misfortune.

The question of whether the commodity is a material thing or an intangible service is irrelevant. Workers in the service sector, provided they create some kind of use-value, material or otherwise, may well be producing surplus value. Marx takes the example of a teacher in a private school run for profit:

> If we may take an example from outside the sphere of production of material objects, a schoolmaster is a productive labourer when, in addition to belabouring the heads of his scholars, he works like a horse to enrich the school proprietor. That the latter has laid out his capital in a teaching factory, instead of in a sausage factory, does not alter the relation.

In his *Theories of Surplus Value* Marx contrasts a clown employed by a capitalist with a self-employed tailor whose services are used by the same capitalist:

> An actor, for example, or even a clown…is a productive labourer if he works in the service of a capitalist…to whom he returns more labour than he receives from him in the form of wages; while a jobbing tailor who comes to the capitalist's house and patches his trousers for him, producing a mere use-value for him, is an unproductive labourer.

Marx points out that in this example the clown's labour is exchanged with capital in order to renew and expand that capital through a production process. The self-employed tailor, by contrast, merely receives some of the surplus value that the capitalist has already gained through their exploitation of the clown. Of course, if a second capitalist employed the tailor for a wage, and so gained surplus value from the business of repairing trousers, then the labour would be productive for that capitalist.

As well as narrowing down the concept of productive labour to those involved in the production of surplus value, Marx also expands it to account for the changing nature of work—involving a "collective labourer" with individuals performing a variety of coordinated tasks:

> As the cooperative character of the labour process becomes more and more marked, so, as a necessary consequence, does our notion of productive labour, and of its agent the productive labourer, become extended.

What of those workers, such as doctors and teachers employed by the state, who do not directly produce surplus value for a capitalist?

Such workers are clearly exploited. In general, the amount of labour they provide exceeds the labour time represented by their wage. Furthermore, the conditions of labour of most such workers, including teachers, nurses and low ranking civil servants, are dictated by conditions in the wider working class. Indeed, the experience of working in a large school, hospital or job centre is little different from working in a factory or office. These workers are subject to the same pressures and are equally capable of resisting them. They are also potentially extremely powerful because they are essential to the production of surplus value in the wider economy.

For instance, they play a vital role in reproducing labour power. So Marx writes in his *Theories of Surplus Value*:

> As to the purchase of such services as those which train labour power, maintain or modify it, etc, in a word, give it a specialised form or even only maintain it—thus for example the schoolmaster's service, in so far as it is "industrially necessary" or useful;

the doctor's service in so far as he maintains health and so conserves the source of all values, labour power itself—these are services which yield in return...a commodity...namely labour power itself, into whose costs of production or reproduction these services enter.

Immediately after this passage Marx points out the limited extent of such expenditure in the capitalism of his day. The same is not true of contemporary capitalism, in which state expenditures on health and education constitute a large chunk of the economy in most countries.

Such labour is not directly productive in the strict sense. For instance, it is generally paid for through state revenue generated out of wages, profits and other taxable income—rather than paying for itself and generating surplus value through a process of capitalist production and the subsequent sale of commodities. Nonetheless it is a vital prerequisite for production to take place at all and should therefore be understood as part of the wider collective labour process required if society is to produce surplus value.

The reserve army of labour

FOR many in capitalist society the one thing worse than being exploited is not being exploited. The poverty faced by many pensioners, who are no longer useful to the capitalists, or those whose health, mental or physical, makes them less useful to the capitalists is an indictment of a system build around the extraction of surplus value. But capitalism also creates vast numbers of unemployed who are perfectly willing and able to work, and who are potentially useful to capitalism in creating surplus value.

Mechanisation and automation, which replace workers with machinery, the ebbs and flows of the "business cycle", and attempts by capitalists to make existing workers work harder (part of the process of "downsizing") all create pools of unemployment. Some earlier writers had argued that biological factors—the uncontrolled growth of the population—were the key to explaining this "overpopulation". So Thomas Malthus, an influential economist in Marx's time, argued that population would always grow faster than the food supply, leading to the impoverishment of a section of the population.

Marx, by contrast, argues that the process of capitalist development itself creates a "surplus population" expelled from production. At the same time, this surplus population becomes a "lever" for the future development of capitalism:

> It forms a disposable industrial reserve army, that belongs to capital quite as absolutely as if the latter

had bred it at its own cost. Independently of the limits of the actual increase of population, it creates, for the changing needs of the self-expansion of capital, a mass of human material always ready for exploitation.

The existence of this "reserve army" of labour also disciplines employed workers. Wages tend to fluctuate around average levels, Marx argues, with the ebb and flow of various branches of production. This helps draw workers into expanding areas while expelling them from those that are contracting. But the threat of unemployment places limits on the average level of wages:

> If, eg, in consequence of favourable circumstances, accumulation in a particular sphere of production becomes especially active, and profits in it, being greater than the average profits, attract additional capital, of course the demand for labour rises and wages also rise. The higher wages draw a larger part of the working population into the more favoured sphere, until it is glutted with labour power, and wages at length fall again to their average level or below it, if the pressure is too great. Then not only does the immigration of labourers into the branch of industry in question cease; it gives place to their emigration...
>
> The industrial reserve army, during the periods of stagnation and average prosperity, weighs down the active labour army; during the periods of overproduction and paroxysm it holds its pretensions in check. Relative surplus population is therefore the pivot upon which the law of demand and supply of labour works. It confines the field of action of this law within the limits absolutely convenient to the activity of exploitation and to the domination of capital.

Unravelling Capitalism

Of course, from the standpoint of meeting human needs, the existence of unemployed workers who wish to work is completely irrational. If there is a mass of unused bricks and mortar, unemployed labourers and people who require somewhere to live, from a socialist point of view the solution is very simple indeed. But within a system built on profit and the extraction of surplus value from workers, unemployment is perfectly rational.

A world of alienation

CAPITALISM degrades the worker—and not simply through the injustice of exploitation, which was, in a different form, also the fate of the peasant in feudal England or the slave in ancient Rome. Long before he wrote *Capital*, Marx had a number of insights into "human nature" that form a crucial complement to his later work.

Most earlier thinkers, if they considered human nature at all, imagined it to be a fixed, unchanging thing. Marx saw it as rooted in a process that gave rise to change and dynamism—labour. Human beings become distinct from animals once they consciously labour on their environment to meet their needs. This process of labour is collective and social. Humans enter into "definite social relations independent of their will" to produce. So the earliest hunter-gatherers, if they were to be successful in hunting, had to cooperate and develop forms of communication. This is not simply a genetic impulse or instinct, even if humans' particular biology makes it possible. Some animals (bees or ants) build complex colonies, but these are fixed in advance by their genetic make-up. Humans, by contrast, can change how they labour through a conscious and reflective process. So Marx writes:

> A spider conducts operations that resemble those of a weaver, and a bee puts to shame many an architect in the construction of her cells. But what distinguishes

the worst architect from the best of bees is this, that the architect raises his structure in imagination before he erects it in reality.

Humans are in tension with the rest of nature. They have to labour to transform it in order to survive. But the process also transforms humans as society develops. Labour, for Marx, is the foundation of society. But the development of the labour process—the relationship between humans and nature—is far from straightforward. At a certain point in history, Marx argues, classes develop. A section of society frees itself from the necessity to labour directly and begins to control any surplus wealth generated by society. This group eventually establishes itself as a ruling class.

Accompanying this process of class division is another called "alienation"—the systematic distortion of the labour process. This in turn means the distortion of the relationship of humans to nature and of relationships among humans. Under capitalism alienation takes on a particularly extreme form. For example, the worker, as we have seen, is compelled to sell their labour power to a capitalist. The process of labour and the object of labour become "alien" things. The worker no longer has any control over the conditions of their labour or the products their labour produces. Because the labour process is central to what constitutes human beings, alienation also means that the worker is alienated from their own nature. Indeed, the worker is dominated by alien products of labour—machinery, computers, and so on. This process of alienation is closely connected to another of Marx's concepts that we have already encountered: commodity fetishism, the way that real relationships between humans present themselves as market relationships between things.

Some Marxists have argued that, while alienation was of interest to the "young Marx", the "mature Marx" who wrote *Capital* was more interested in the objective laws of the capitalist economy. But the theme of alienation is present in *Capital* and especially in the *Grundrisse*. Here Marx writes of "the alien quality of the objective conditions of labour that confront living labour capacity, which goes so far that these conditions confront the person of the worker in the person of the capitalist—as personification with its own will and interest". The worker's labour "appears as *alien labour*"; the products of past labour take on the form of "*things, values*", which appear to the workers "in an alien, commanding personification".

This process has a degrading affect on workers because:

the worker emerges not only not richer, but emerges rather poorer from the process than he entered. For not only has he produced the conditions of necessary labour as conditions belonging to capital; but also the value-creating possibility...which lies as a possibility within him, now likewise exists as surplus value...in a word as capital, as master over living labour capacity, as value endowed with its own might and will, confronting him in his abstract, objectless, purely subjective poverty.

Marx does not develop these notions in order to show that workers are somehow trapped in a prison of alienation and commodity fetishism. His central point is that this condition arose at a point in history and can be changed in the future. Indeed, capitalism, for the first time, provides the possibility for humans to overcome alienation and exploitation. Capitalism provides the basis for socialism: a world of unalienated labour, under democratic control, in which production is geared towards meeting an expanding range of human needs.

It provides the basis for this in two senses. First, it is the most dynamic society ever. It creates the wealth sufficient to abolish scarcity and so the necessity of class division. The potential exists today for a world in which humanity's ever expanding needs—cultural and intellectual needs as well as basic material needs—could be met, even if this potential is constantly undercut by the reality of a system based on class division and market competition. Second, it creates a global working class composed of millions of people in homogenous conditions, forced to struggle against their exploitation, who through their own actions could create a socialist society.

Workers can hold distorted ideas such as racism or sexism. But these are always in tension with another set of ideas generated by collective experiences of struggle. Racist ideas, for example, can rapidly be transcended if white workers are forced to fight alongside and in solidarity with black colleagues. Groups of unskilled women workers in Britain at the end of the 19th century challenged sexist preconceptions through a series of militant strikes. Women workers striking in Egypt in recent years have done the same.

Not only does class struggle under capitalism overcome divisions between workers; it also lays the basis for a novel way of running society. Working class struggle has a different character to that of earlier struggles. In the feudal world peasants could rise up, seize the land (the source of most wealth) and divide it up to farm in the old way.

Under capitalism class struggle takes on a different form. You cannot divide up a supermarket, factory or hospital. The solutions discovered by the working class tend to be democratic and collective solutions. This is the essence of socialist revolution—it is the self-emancipation of workers through their own collective, conscious struggle. Capitalism opens up the historical possibility that alienation can be transcended. Not only that, but the frequent crises thrown up by the capitalist system during its frenzied development call its continued existence into question.

The next section of this work will explain why capitalism has such great dynamism and consider how this generates repeated economic crises.

Part 2

DYNAMICS OF THE SYSTEM

The circulation of capital

So far I have focused on the "sphere of production"—the realm in which workers are exploited, values produced and surplus value grabbed by the capitalist. I have done so in a way that "abstracts" from the surface appearance of the system to grasp its innermost laws. For Marx what happens in production is crucial to the overall dynamics of the system, even if capitalist commentators do not realise this. They tend instead to be fixated on the spheres of exchange (the purchase and sale of commodities on the market) and distribution (in which surplus value is shared out and redistributed among capitalists). The second and third volumes of *Capital* are increasingly concerned with drawing together production, exchange and distribution to develop a more concrete picture of the system as a whole.

Marx views capitalism as a constantly evolving process in which capital circulates through the system. In analysing this circuit, it is possible to start at any point. If the starting point is money, then this money must be advanced to purchase commodities— labour power, raw materials, machinery, etc. These commodities are then used in production. The process of production creates new commodities and these are then sold for money. Marx represents this cycle using symbols:

M—C..P..C'—M'

M = money at start; C = commodities used in production;
P = production process; C' = produced commodities;
M' = money at end

Starting from money, or M, gives one particular window on how capitalism works. From the point of view of the capitalist the important thing is that M' is greater than M. The capitalist wants to end up with more money than they started with. Here the process of production (where surplus value is actually created) seems almost incidental. It appears as if the capitalist could equally buy products cheap and sell them dear to make money. This is similar to the way that merchants operate, which was very important early in the history of capitalism. They could exploit price differences in different areas to make a profit, especially if they were able to transport commodities over large distances, for instance spices brought from the Far East by ship. This would be represented by: M—C—M'. Note the similarity to the circuit above. From this standpoint everything is mystified.

To take an even more mystifying example, the capitalist could simply take their money and lend it to earn interest. This could be represented by M—M'. It appears as if capital is expanding of its own accord. This is a particularly extreme version of the "fetishism of commodities" discussed at the beginning of this book. We will see later how this mysterious expansion is actually a redistribution of surplus value from one point in the system to another.

There are other windows through which we can look at capitalism. For instance, if we start and finish with production rather than money, the circuit of capital looks like this:

P..C'—M'—C..P

Now the process of exchange represents an interruption to the production process. The question becomes, how does the capitalist rapidly sell their commodities on the market and restart the production process anew?

Looking at the circuit of capital also raises the question of what happens to the expanded portion of capital, the extra money that M' constitutes over and above M—the surplus value pumped out of workers.

Marx considers two possibilities. The first is what he calls "simple reproduction". Here Marx assumes that capitalists personally consume all of the surplus value they pump out of workers. He further assumes that capitalists buy the same kind of wage goods that workers buy. In this model the economy can therefore be divided into two "departments". Department 1 produces means of production—the raw materials, machinery, etc—which are purchased by capitalists to use as constant capital. Department 2 produces "means of consumption"—the basic consumption goods that workers buy with their wages (and, in this model, capitalists also buy using the surplus value they have seized). It is possible to work out a precise mathematical relationship between the capitals flowing through the different sectors of the economy that would allow it to reproduce itself over and over again.

In the second, more complicated, model, "expanded reproduction", Marx assumes that the surplus value is used by the capitalists to purchase more means of production and expand their output. Again it is possible to look mathematically at how the two departments would have to coexist in order to allow production to expand in a smooth, orderly manner.

These two "reproduction schemas", as they have become known, should be treated with great caution. Marx is not attempting to show the conditions for the harmonious development of capitalism. The schemas are more "abstractions". They show the way that capitalism must draw complex individual processes together into a cycle of production and exchange in order to reproduce itself, and they show the instability of the system. The exact proportions required for even growth are never achieved, because capitalism is an unplanned and anarchic system of market competition and uncoordinated decisions taken by individual capitalists and states. And it is a system that changes over time, disturbing any possible equilibrium long before it is achieved.

The reproduction schemas and the circuit of capitalism that Marx sketches in the second volume of *Capital* also indicate the possibility of capitalism "breaking down". The circuit could potentially break down at any of several points. Commodities could remain unsold (C'—M' breaks down). Or the capitalists could panic about whether they can make a profit and refuse to purchase inputs, preferring to invest their money elsewhere (C—M breaks down). Or, equally, some problem in the process of production, say a strike, can interrupt the circuit. Already we see the abstract possibility of economic crisis; later we will see how laws of motion of capitalism lead the system towards such a crisis again and again.

In showing this abstract possibility of crisis Marx is challenging the law developed by Jean-Baptiste Say, an earlier French economist. As Say put it, "A product is no sooner created, than it, from that instant, affords a market for other products to the full extent of its own value." Say's law was interpreted by many economists as saying that supply creates demand. The more capitalists produce and sell goods, the greater the demand for inputs becomes. As John Stuart Mill wrote, in his attempt to popularise Say's law:

All sellers are inevitably, and by the meaning of the word, buyers. Could we suddenly double the productive powers of the country, we should double the supply of commodities in every market; but we should, by the same stroke, double the purchasing power.

And so, for Say and Mill, a glut of unsold commodities is impossible and there can be no "generalised overproduction". But, as Marx argues, the capitalist is not exchanging products for products: "It is not only a question of replacing *the same* quantity of use-values of which capital consists, on the former scale or on an enlarged scale...but of replacing the *value* of the capital advanced along with the usual rate of profit (surplus value)." Marx writes:

> Nothing could be more childish than the dogma, that because every sale is a purchase, and every purchase a sale, therefore the circulation of commodities necessarily implies an equilibrium of sale and purchase... No one can sell unless someone else purchases. But no one is forthwith bound to purchase because he has just sold... If the split between the sale and the purchase becomes too pronounced, the intimate connection between them, their oneness, asserts itself by producing—a crisis.

For example, any fall in the prices of commodities, for whatever reason, can curtail the reproduction of capital. And the fact that money plays its role in circulation means there is little incentive for the capitalist to invest in these circumstances:

> surplus value amassed in the form of money...could only be transformed into capital at a loss. It therefore

lies idle as a hoard... The same hold up could occur for the opposite reasons, if the *real prerequisites* of reproduction were missing... There occurs a stoppage in reproduction, and thus in the flow of circulation. Purchase and sale get bogged down and unemployed capital appears in the form of idle money.

Once this sort of situation takes hold, it can spread from sector to sector of the economy. If a newspaper proprietor cuts production, that in turn affects paper suppliers and printing press manufacturers; if workers are laid off, it affects capitalists who produce basic foodstuffs and clothing, and so on. Generalised overproduction, the production of too much output, becomes possible. This is another irrational aspect of capitalist production. In 1997 a crisis broke out in South East Asia, in part because there was overproduction of computer equipment. It did not mean that everyone who wanted a computer had one. Overproduction merely means that nobody wishes to buy goods at the price they command or that they do not have the money to back up their need. Under capitalism it is value rather than need that counts.

Marx did not stop once he had shown that it was possible for crisis to spread through the capitalist system. It still remains to show *how* crisis develops, what form it takes, and so on. Much of the rest of this book will examine this.

Considering the circulation of capital also leads us to another question—that of the "turnover" of capital. The time taken for capital to turn over is the time it spends in the spheres of production and of circulation. "It is the period of time from the moment of the advance of capital-value in a definite form to the return of the functioning capital-value in the same form." Obviously this will vary vastly under different circumstances.

In our example of newspaper production, the ink and paper should (in good market conditions) turn over relatively quickly. They are purchased and thrown into the production process. They circulate through the value they add to the newspaper. Once the newspaper is sold money returns to the capitalist. The capitalist can then advance the money as capital to purchase more ink and paper. However, the value of the printing press will turn over much more slowly, taking years or even decades to complete. In general, fixed capital will turn over more slowly than circulating capital. It gradually returns to the capitalist in the form of money. So the circulating capital will turn over several times during the period required for the fixed capital to turn over.

This raises some problems in comparing different capitals. Marx points out that two different capitals can be compared if one looks at the amount of capital turned over in a given period in money form. For example, suppose the fixed capital is £80,000 and its period of reproduction ten years, so that £8,000 is annually returned to its money form (so it completes one tenth of its turnover each year). Suppose further the circulating capital is £20,000, and its turnover is completed five times per year. The total capital would then be £100,000. The turned over fixed capital is £8,000, the turned over circulating capital five times £20,000, or £100,000. Then the capital turned over during one year is £108,000 or £8,000 more than the advanced capital. $1 + {}^2\!/_{25}$ of the capital has been turned over.

The turnover time of capital is of crucial importance to the capitalists. The faster they can make their capital turn over, the more rapidly they can begin another cycle of production and thus generate more surplus value.

Consider two capitalists are engaged in identical processes of production employing equal quantities of capital. The first turns over all their capital in six months, the second in a year. Over the course of the year the first capitalist can turn over twice as much capital. Thus they can extract twice as much surplus value. Clearly there will be great pressure on capitalists to decrease their turnover time—in other words, to turn over their capital as frequently as possible in a given period of time.

Capital's self-expansion

THERE is no virtue in the capitalist getting £1 million in profit a year if they have to invest £1 billion in capital to get it. At that rate it would take 1,000 years to acquire enough profit for them to double the size of their business. Capitalists are not interested in the *amount* of profit; they are interested in the return on investment—how many pennies they get back for each pound they invest. This is what Marx calls the "rate of profit". It is the rate of "self-expansion" of capital, the rate at which it grows. Based on the assumptions made so far, we can easily work this out. It is simply the surplus value pumped out of workers in a given period, divided by the amount of capital invested in labour power, means of production and so on:

Rate of profit = surplus value / (constant capital + variable capital)

Returning to the example of the newspaper manufacturer we considered earlier, we learned that, in a day, the total value produced was £2,400 and that this could be broken down into surplus value, constant capital and variable capital:

Total value of day's output
= 1,600 hours of constant capital + 400 hours of variable capital
+ 400 hours of surplus value
= £1,600 constant capital + £400 variable capital
+ £400 surplus value
= £2,400

So, in this example, the rate of profit for the day is:

Rate of profit = surplus value / (constant capital + variable capital)

$= \quad {}^{400}/_{(1600\ +\ 400)} = {}^{400}/_{2000}$

$= \quad {}^1/_5$

In other words, here the capitalist's rate of profit is 20 percent, or 20p in profit for every £1 they invest.

The rate of profit is actually a slightly strange way of looking at things. Surplus value is compared to both constant capital (raw material, machinery, etc) and variable capital (wages). But we know that it is only living labour (paid for by wages) that creates surplus value. This is another example of commodity fetishism—the mystified way that capitalism presents itself—because it appears to the capitalist as if *all* of their capital is creating surplus value. Nonetheless this is exactly how the capitalist sees things. The rate of profit is the rate of self-expansion of capital, which, as we shall see, is central to the logic of capitalism.

Accumulate, accumulate!

TOWARDS the end of the first volume of *Capital* Marx writes, "Hitherto we have investigated how surplus value emanates from capital; we have now to see how capital arises from surplus value. Employing surplus value as capital, reconverting it into capital, is called accumulation of capital."

This process, the accumulation of capital, is the most unique feature of the capitalist system and it is crucial to understanding its dynamic. We have already seen how capitalism is distinguished from earlier societies by the special way that surplus value, unpaid for labour time, is extracted from workers. But this is not the only unique feature of capitalism. Capitalism is also a system of market competition. Production is geared towards the market and this forms the terrain for competition between different capitalists. In other words, there are two key divisions in capitalist society: one between workers and capitalists, and another dividing the capitalists from other capitalists. And there is another difference with previous forms of society. Under capitalism the drive to exploit workers, extract surplus value and use it to expand production—to accumulate—is unlimited. In pre-capitalist societies the limits of exploitation were imposed by the walls of the rulers' stomachs. Once the luxury consumption of these rulers and the basic needs of those they ruled over were met, there was no great drive to produce more. But under capitalism this is not so, because the bulk of the new value created is accumulated—it is ploughed back into the production process with the aim of creating ever more profit.

This process of competitive accumulation of capital is both the central driving force of capitalism and the source of many of its problems—making it both extremely dynamic and extremely prone to crises.

Accumulation itself is a simple enough concept. Capitalists turn some of their surplus value into new capital. This might mean a simple expansion of production in which the capitalist uses some of the surplus value to hire more workers and buy more machinery and raw material, ie purchasing more of the same kinds of constant and variable capital. But it might also mean investment in new technology that makes production more efficient. This is an extremely important form of accumulation because it allows capitalists to compete more effectively with rival capitalists.

Marx writes in *Capital*, "The battle of competition is fought by cheapening of commodities. The cheapness of commodities depends...on the productivity of labour." As more and better technology is set in motion by each worker, so more commodities can be produced with less labour time—and because value reflects labour time the cost of those commodities will fall.

In an earlier example we used, we imagined that newspapers produced by a capitalist had a value of three hours worth of labour time. If each hour is worth £1, the newspaper is worth £3. Now imagine that the capitalist finds a way to make workers more productive without having to invest any more, meaning that now ten newspapers can be produced in the same period. Now each is only worth 30p—the same labour time, and so the same value, is split between a greater number of commodities. The capitalist with the most productive workers can produce the goods most cheaply and undercut rival capitalists.

In practice, raising productivity generally means bringing in new, and typically more expensive, technology. Often it also means getting rid of workers. This pattern first became clear in Britain's Industrial Revolution. For instance, in the textile industry the invention of Samuel Crompton's spinning "mule" in 1779 made it possible for one spinner to produce as much thread as 200 workers had previously produced, destroying the jobs of hand spinners. Later, from 1813 onwards, mechanical looms began to drive out hand weaving in a similar way.

Marx is interested in the way different types and quantities of living labour (the labour of workers) and dead labour (machinery and raw materials) are brought together in factories and other workplaces. He refers to the way they are brought together as the "technical composition of capital". This is simply a comparison of different use-values, for instance, 200 spinners brought together with 200 spinning wheels and 200 yards of thread, or one spinner brought together with one spinning mule and 200 yards of thread.

How can the impact of changes in this technical composition of capital on the dynamic of the system be measured? The answer is by looking at the values set in motion—what value of labour power is brought together with what value of machinery and raw materials. Marx develops two different ways of measuring this. The most straightforward is what he calls the "value composition" of capital. This is simply the ratio of the value of all of the inputs of constant capital to the value of the inputs of variable capital.

Value composition = constant capital / variable capital

Unravelling Capitalism

Let's say that Crompton's spinning mule costs £1,000, an old fashioned spinning wheel costs £1, unspun thread costs £1 per yard and labour costs £10 per worker over the period taken to spin the thread. Consider spinning 200 yards of thread.

So, before Crompton developed his spinning mule:

c = [value of 200 spinning wheels] + [value of 200 yards of thread]
   = [200 x 1] + [200 x 1] = £400
v = [value of 200 wages]
   = [200 x 10] = £2,000

c = constant capital; v = variable capital

The initial value composition is:

$2000/400 = 5$

After the spinning mule is developed:

c = [value of one spinning mule] + [value of 200 yards of thread]
   = [1,000] + [200 x 1] = £1,200
v = [value of one wage]
   = £10

The new value composition is:

$1200/10 = 120$

In other words, the value composition has risen dramatically. A far greater value of dead labour, or constant capital, is set in motion per worker. The expensive investment makes sense because the spun thread is cheaper—less labour time is embodied in each yard of thread.

But Marx is also aware that the value composition of capital is a very unstable quantity. The thread used in the spinning process and the spinning mule or spinning wheels are themselves commodities, bought by the capitalist. We can expect that these things will also get cheaper as capitalism develops. We can also expect the wage to contain less and less value as the goods bought by the worker cheapen. This means that the value composition will change over time, even if exactly the same techniques are used in the industry under investigation.

Marx is interested in being able to measure the changes that come about simply as a result of technological innovation in a particular industry. In other words, he wants to be able to measure just those changes brought about by alterations in the technological composition of capital, not the fluctuating price of raw material, machinery and wage goods. In order to do this he introduces a different measure, which he calls the "organic composition of capital". This is the same as the value composition except that it ignores changes in the prices of the inputs into the production process. In other words, the organic composition mirrors directly changes to the technical composition, while the value composition also reflects wider changes taking place in other branches of the economy. As Marx writes:

> The composition of capital is to be understood in a two-fold sense. On the side of value, it is determined by the proportion in which it is divided into constant capital or value of the means of production, and variable capital or value of labour power, the sum total of wages. On the side of material, as it functions in the process of production, all capital is divided into means of production and living labour power. This

Unravelling Capitalism

latter composition is determined by the relation between the mass of the means of production employed, on the one hand, and the mass of labour necessary for their employment on the other. I call the former the *value composition*, the latter the *technical composition of capital*. Between the two there is a strict correlation. To express this, I call the value composition of capital, in so far as it is determined by its technical composition and mirrors the changes of the latter, the *organic composition of capital*.

We will see later why the distinction is important. But for now we will imagine that the two measures of the composition of capital are the same as we consider the impact of raising the organic composition of capital through investment.

The falling rate of profit

How does the rising organic composition of capital brought about by accumulation affect the capitalist? Let us consider another example from the print industry. The technology used in printing presses has changed considerably in recent decades. Each worker operates an ever greater accumulation of dead labour. Twenty years ago this book could have been produced on a printing press that cost £350,000, operated by one printer. Today this press has been replaced by one costing £2 million, still operated by a single printer. The capitalist invests much more but the new press is more productive so it can print more books and at a faster rate, reducing the value embodied in each individual book. If each book is cheaper, the capitalist can compete successfully with rivals who are still using old technology.

A simple example will demonstrate this. Imagine that a number of capitalists are involved in producing books. Each of them has to put forward £10 constant capital (machinery, raw material, etc) and £10 variable capital (wages) each day. And imagine they get £10 surplus value (profit) from the exploitation of their workers each day. Finally, they each produce ten books each day. Then the total value produced by a particular capitalist each day is £30. There are ten books, so each book has a value of £3.

Now, what happens if one of these capitalists invests in new technology? They still pay £10 wages and get £10 surplus value, but now they pay £20 instead of

£10 in constant capital. But their new technique is far more productive—instead of producing ten books they produce 100 each day. Now the capitalist who innovated is producing £40 of value each day instead of £30. But they have 100 books, not ten. So less value is embodied in each individual book. Each book is now worth just 40p (instead of £3). In the short term the capitalist making this investment wins out over their rivals. They can flood the market and charge slightly less than £3 per book but much more than the 40p of value embodied in it. But eventually the other capitalists will be forced to try to innovate and pretty soon they too will be involved in price cutting to compete. Over time the price of each book will fall to somewhere around its value of 40p. In the process some of the capitalists, presumably the ones who fail to innovate rapidly enough and therefore cannot cut their prices, will be driven out of business.

This is how competitive accumulation works. But if we look closely at the figures, something very strange has happened. With the old technology the capitalists got £10 surplus value from £20 investment (£10 wages and £10 constant capital). Their rate of profit using the old technique was, therefore, 50 percent. With the new technology they still get £10 surplus value, but their investment is now £30. So their new rate of profit is 33 ⅓ percent.

The process of accumulation has driven down the rate of profit. Why is this? The capitalists raised productivity by raising the organic composition of capital—by making each worker harness a greater value of constant capital, or dead labour. But the amount of living labour stayed the same. A greater and greater mass of dead labour is used compared to living labour. Machinery and computers replace workers, or at the least, their use grows at a more rapid pace. Living labour is expelled from the production process relative to dead labour. But we have learned that living labour is the source of surplus value. So the capitalist, in the struggle to get more profit, drives out the very thing that generates profit.

Why would any capitalist behave in this way? First, we should note that capitalists do not know where their surplus value comes from. For them it seems to come as much from printing presses as it does from workers. Second, for the first capitalist who innovates it makes perfect sense. They can carry on selling their books just below the old price even though there is far less value embodied in each one. In other words, for a time they will enjoy an incredibly high rate of profit. It is only in the long term, when other capitalists innovate and competition forces prices down, that the overall impact of accumulation is felt.

This is a contradiction at the heart of the capitalist system—the perfectly rational decisions of individual capitalists, taken to satisfy their short-term interests, when copied by other equally rational capitalists, lead to utterly irrational long-term consequences for the system as a whole.

The great irony is that surplus value is what allows capitalists to accumulate. But accumulation in turn leads to falling profit rates and makes further accumulation difficult.

This revelation was, for Marx, "in every respect the most important law of modern political economy". He called it the "law of the tendency of the rate of profit to fall" and it plays a central role in his theory of capitalist crisis. As Marx put it, "The rate of self-expansion of capitalism, or the rate of profit, being the goal of capitalist production, its fall...appears as a threat to the capitalist production process." The threat to accumulation comes from accumulation itself:

Unravelling Capitalism

The real barrier of capitalist production is capital it-self. It is the fact that capital and its self-expansion appear as the starting and closing point, as the motive and aim of production; that production is merely production for capital... Thus, while the capitalist mode of production is one of the historical means by which the material forces of production are developed and the world market required for them created, it is at the same time in continual conflict with this historical task and the conditions of social production corresponding to it.

Once the rate of accumulation slows, the system as a whole struggles to consume all that it creates. If workers cannot afford to purchase the output of the system, because their consumption is restricted by the level of their wage, and capitalists do not expect to make enough profit to justify investing, the result can be generalised overproduction.

Escape seems impossible for the capitalists because the system contains at its heart a drive to accumulate. Capitalists do not squeeze workers and pump the surplus value back into production out of personal malice or greed—although it is perfectly possible for both to motivate particular capitalists. They do so because if they do not they will be driven to the wall. The competition between capitalists forces them to behave as capitalists. This is one fundamental reason why "ethical capitalism" is a dead end—in a world of competitive accumulation the capitalist is forced to stop being ethical or stop being a capitalist.

The drive to accumulate makes capitalism dynamic and destructive in a way never seen before. It is dynamic because there is a constant battle to raise the productivity of labour. As Marx and Engels wrote in their *Communist*

Manifesto of 1848, "The bourgeoisie cannot exist without constantly revolutionising the means of production." This massive growth in the potential material wealth of society was, for Marx, one of the things that made a socialist world an objective possibility.

But accumulation is also a destructive force. Anything that poses an obstacle to accumulation must be destroyed—whether it is the cost of pensions for retired workers, workplace safety laws or even the environment. As Marx puts it, "Accumulate, accumulate! That is Moses and the prophets... Accumulation for accumulation's sake, production for production's sake." As if this were not bad enough, accumulation is now seen to be self-defeating, a barrier to further accumulation. Capitalism is not simply an inequitable and unpleasant system; it is one riven with internal contradictions.

Counteracting influences

IF the rate of profit simply dropped like a stone, capitalism would have long since collapsed. Clearly other forces are at work. Marx is sometimes portrayed as a kind of prophet of doom—predicting the system's inevitable collapse into an inescapable economic crisis and the equally inevitable rise of a socialist society on its ruins. In fact neither is inevitable. And Marx, immediately after developing his "law of the tendency of the rate of profit to fall" in volume three of *Capital*, describes the "counteracting influences" that will tend to restore profit rates or even increase them for a time. It is, for Marx, these counteracting influences that turn the "law" of the falling rate of profit into a mere "tendency":

> If we consider the enormous development of the productive forces of social labour in the last 30 years alone as compared with all preceding periods…then the difficulty which has hitherto troubled the economist, namely to explain the falling rate of profit, gives place to its opposite, namely to explain why this fall is not greater and more rapid. There must be some counteracting influences at work, which cross and annul the effect of the general law, and which give it merely the characteristic of a tendency.

Marx lists a whole number of possible counteracting influences, but some are particularly important. One we have already encountered. This is for the capitalists to simply increase the degree of exploitation of their workers. This could mean lengthening the working day or cutting pay, or it could take place through the gradual cheapening of the goods the workers buy with their wage. We encountered these as examples of increasing "absolute" and "relative" surplus value.

However, as we saw, there are limits to these processes. The working day cannot be longer than 24 hours (and it cannot even be that long without crippling or killing the worker). Similarly, there are limits to the process of cheapening labour power and so increasing the share of the working day going to the production of surplus value. The mathematical limit for this is for the workers to produce a whole working day's worth of surplus value and nothing towards their wages, but again there are physical limits (such as the starvation of the worker) before this point is reached.

There is another important counteracting influence: the cheapening of the constant capital used in production. We have seen how productivity rises brought about by accumulation have two effects. They tend to reduce the rate of profit and they also reduce the price of commodities. Some of these commodities, for example machinery, are also means of production. This is why Marx distinguishes the organic composition of capital (which ignores this cheapening of the inputs) from the value composition (which takes it into account). By focusing on the organic composition, Marx can concentrate on the tendency for the rate of profit to fall; turning to the value composition, he can look at the counteracting influences.

To show how the cheapening of inputs can raise the rate of profit we can go back to the example we used earlier. We considered a book manufacturer who advanced £10 variable capital and £10 constant capital, and received £10 of surplus value produced by the workers. This gives the capitalist a rate of profit of $10/20 = \frac{1}{2} = 50$ percent. Now, if the cost of the constant capital falls to £5 because of technical progress in a different branch of the economy, the new rate of profit is $10/15 = \frac{2}{3} = 66 \frac{2}{3}$ percent.

However, the devaluation of machinery and raw materials has a contradictory impact on accumulation for two reasons. First, boosting profit rates in this way means that a greater amount of surplus value is freed up. But where does that surplus value go? We have already seen how capitalists are driven to accumulate their surplus value. So, having invested in cheaper means of production, the temptation for the capitalists will be to invest what is left over in yet more accumulation. Often this will mean simply raising the organic composition of capital in new ways. It is relatively easy for all capitalists in a given sector of the economy to take advantage of techniques that require cheaper means of production. But the most successful capitalists will be those who *also* have access to all those techniques that require *more expensive* means of production. The number of such innovations and techniques is potentially unlimited.

In practice, most capitalists realise that they will be more competitive if they are able to make large-scale investments. So a June 2007 article in the *Financial Times* lamented a recent decline in the "amount of capital that European and US companies are willing to spend on factories and equipment". Such spending, it continued, has been "the traditional engine of profit and economic growth".

The drive to invest surplus value in search of more surplus value means that for the cheapening of constant capital to have a sustained restorative impact on profit rates it is necessary to have some kind of outlet that draws off the surplus value freed up. Some kind of "leak" out of the capitalist circuit of production is required— some way of destroying, wasting or hoarding this value, so preventing it from being reinvested in another round of accumulation.

The second problem with this counteracting influence is that it often hurts particular capitalists as much as it helps them. For instance, if a capitalist has just bought a £2 million printing press, and someone comes along and develops a £1 million version of the same machine, it does not help the capitalist who has already invested. They still have to pay for their £2 million machine. Their competitors, meanwhile, who were slower to invest, will enjoy the benefit of a cheaper machine. And these competitors will be able to produce commodities even more cheaply, undercutting the capitalist lumbered with the £2 million press. This sort of process, which Marx called the "moral depreciation" of capital, becomes as painful for the capitalist as the falling rate of profit.

In fact neither the law of the tendency of the rate of profit to fall nor the counteracting tendencies give rise to smooth, gradual and predictable trends. Instead the system develops through chaotic expansion interrupted by sudden crises.

Indeed, historically the most effective way of restoring profit rates has been the crises that resolve the tensions and contradictions that build up in the economy. During a crisis some capitalists are driven out of business. Those that remain can grab their unused capital at bargain prices. Commodities are piled up in warehouses and can be bought at a fraction of their value. Large amounts of surplus value are destroyed, but what remains is shared between fewer capitalists. Finally, wages tend to be driven down by unemployment, so labour power cheapens.

In short, a crisis devalues capital on a vast scale, allowing the system to restore or even raise its profitability, at least for a time. It is this kind of devaluation of capital, rather than the slow cheapening of inputs into production, that is most effective in allowing capitalism to continue driving forwards. We must now look at how capitalist crises develop.

Capitalism and crisis

THERE are three basic approaches to understanding economic crises. The first is the position of the classical theorists of the 19th century who first sought to understand the workings of capitalism. They held that the system was essentially self-regulating, leading to some kind of equilibrium. Adam Smith, one of the greatest of these classical theorists, spoke of the capitalist being led as if by the "invisible hand" of the market: "By pursuing his own interest he frequently promotes that of the society more effectually than when he really intends to promote it."

The neoclassical economists who followed, and reigned supreme right through to the 1930s, rejected Smith and David Ricardo's attempts at a labour theory of value. Instead they based their theories on the ideas of marginalism that concentrated on fluctuations in market prices driven by changes in supply and demand, which could be understood through mathematical techniques. But they accepted much of the classical picture of automatic equilibrium mechanisms. This included Say's law, which we encountered earlier in this book. As the economist John Maynard Keynes wrote of the law in 1936, "The doctrine is never stated today in this crude form. Nevertheless it still underlies the whole...theory, which would collapse without it."

Unfortunately from the classical period through to the 1930s there were regular economic crises, recessions and slowdowns in the major economies. For instance, the National Bureau of Economic Research in the US gives 16 periods of economic contraction from 1854 through to 1919. How were these to be explained?

Often economists turned to external factors, outside of the economy itself, to explain crisis. Perhaps they could be put down to some abnormality of human psychology. Perhaps the problem was the interference of the state in markets—a principle revived by the International Monetary Fund and World Bank in the structural adjustment programmes they imposed on parts of the Third World in the 1980s. One economist, William Stanley Jevons, thought that crises might be caused by sun spots (indeed "sun spots" is the phrase many economists use today to describe how "non-economic" events might cause crises). In all these cases, the economy is seen as a natural, self-regulating system. Some later economists integrated boom and bust into their account by talking about a "business cycle". Capitalism is still self-regulating, but now it goes through a cyclical pattern every ten or so years, rather than simply growing over time. Increasingly such cycles are seen as "natural" phenomena. So one article in the *Observer* in July 2008 described the pattern of recent booms and slumps and went on to talk about the "natural 'business cycle'", as if it could be compared to the turn of the seasons or the tides of the sea.

It was the crisis of the 1930s, which lasted a whole decade, that put paid to this theory. Only mass unemployment, bankruptcy, drastic intervention by states, the carnage of the Second World War and the drive to rearm eventually dragged the system out of the slump. Increasingly a new orthodoxy replaced the old one. This was based on the theory developed by Keynes. Keynes accepted much of the marginalist picture when dealing with the economy at what is today called "the microeconomic level" (the action of individual capitalists and consumers). But he differed in his approach at the "macroeconomic level" (the behaviour of the economy as a whole). According to him, the system tended towards equilibrium, but that equilibrium could be one based on mass unemployment and stagnation or full employment and growth. States had to intervene in the economy by directly investing and stimulating demand to smooth out the business cycle and ensuring the right level of equilibrium.

In the decades following the Second World War it was claimed that "boom and bust" had been eradicated. Unfortunately, from 1945 to 1975 there were seven slowdowns in the US alone, and by the 1970s the world economy was again facing major difficulties. Keynesian solutions, which had not actually been needed for most of the 1950s and 1960s, proved ineffectual in the face of the crisis. Stimulating demand and raising state borrowing to fund investment seemed simply to create spiralling inflation. The Keynesian orthodoxy was ditched. Economists and politicians eventually flipped back to new versions of classical and marginalist theories—monetarism, neoliberalism and so on. Again "boom and bust" were said to be finished. Since then there have been recessions in the US in 1980-2, 1990-1 and 2001-3. As I write this, we are entering a new global downturn—with the first contraction of the world economy since the 1930s—accompanied by much talk of the "end of neoliberalism" and a "return to Keynes".

Marx's theory suggests a different understanding of crisis. For Marxists, capitalism is an unplanned system, based on profit rather than need and competition rather than cooperation. It has internal contradictions that lead to a cycle of boom and bust. But there are also long-term tendencies that can make the booms shorter and shallower, and the recessions longer and more serious. And while Keynesian and classical economics both see capitalism as an eternal system, Marxists, by contrast, see it as a system that emerged at a certain point in history and can end at another—either catastrophically amid poverty and war, or with its overthrow and the establishment of a socialist society.

According to the Marxist picture, the contradictions of capitalism are not worked out smoothly. They lead to recurrent crises, followed by new booms. The business cycle is written into the fabric of capitalism. While the economy is booming, memories of the preceding recession vanish and politicians rush to take credit for a new "golden age". Workers are sucked into jobs, wages can rise as unemployment falls and investment grows. But the boom begins to create conditions for the bust. Competitive accumulation leads to aggressive price-cutting. The least efficient capitalists can be driven under, as can those who invested too early and paid too much for their equipment. At the height of the boom rising labour costs can hit profits and shortages of some goods can create problems, while others, in profitable areas, are overproduced and cannot be sold.

At first just a few companies panic about their profit margins and cut production back. But capitalism is a system in which different producers are linked together through chains of market interactions. What affects one capitalist eventually spreads to the others. As the first capitalist starts cutting back, this hits their suppliers. Eventually companies start laying off workers and demand for consumer goods falls too, hitting more companies. So, for instance, a crisis that begins with a large car firm going bust will first spread to its suppliers, the manufacturers of components such as seatbelts and wing mirrors; then to producers of plastics, metal and glass; and then to supermarkets, bread makers and newspaper printers that depended on all these groups of workers to buy their goods.

But things do not end there. The developing recession creates the conditions for the next boom. As workers are sacked and wages fall, and unprofitable companies are driven under, capital is devalued. Some capitalists go bust or have to sell off goods they have produced at a fraction of their expected price. Workers' wages go down as they face the threat of unemployment. The capitalists that remain can buy up machinery, raw materials and unsold goods, and even take on labour power much more cheaply than before. Eventually the remaining companies feel confident enough to invest and a new boom gets under way. More astute supporters of capitalism are well aware of the possibilities a crisis presents.

A *Financial Times* article by Howard Davies, director of the London School of Economics, in autumn 2008 counselled capitalists on how to deal with a coming recession:

> Current management will need to relearn the fine art of survival. Is all this just a counsel of despair? Not quite. There are positive things that can be done under cover of darkness, so to speak. Companies can more easily generate support for cost-cutting. They can position themselves well for the upturn when it comes, as it will.

In other words, attack workers to boost profits, try to survive the recession and then buy up your rivals as they go under.

The detail of each cycle is different, so to understand each crisis it is necessary to wade through some of the statistics, data and commentary produced by mainstream economists. But it is also important to grasp that boom and bust are based on problems intrinsic to capitalism rather than external factors. The "stop-go" pattern is also a feature of the system when it is in a reasonably healthy state. So during the long boom of the 1950s and 1960s, often referred to as the "golden age" of capitalism, there were still cycles in which the economy grew and then slowed down, even if these were less destructive than at other times.

Sometimes the kind of crisis required to restore the system to "health" is very severe indeed. The rate of profit might be partially restored in a crisis, but usually not to its rate during the preceding boom. So, while profits rise and fall during the cycle, the average profit rate can decline from cycle to cycle, as happened in the period after the Second World War as the organic composition of capital grew gradually over two decades. A full restoration of profit rates might require a very serious crisis, for instance the deep slump of the 1930s, which saw the destruction of vast amounts of capital through economic collapse and global war. Only this, together with the increased state control of economies as they armed for and engaged in the war, could pave the way for a recovery of the rate of profit and lay the basis for a new boom.

An ageing system

THERE is another reason why the cycle of boom and bust does not simply repeat itself over and over again. As capitalism ages it changes. Over time the units of capital, the companies involved, tend to get bigger. The revenue of the 100 biggest corporations in the world is now over $10 trillion, equal to the gross domestic product (GDP) of the 174 poorest countries (out of 195). These giants, many of them multinationals with a global reach, represent a vast accumulation of wealth in a tiny number of hands. Many of the corporations at the top of the league share the same personnel on their boards of directors, making the concentration of wealth and power even greater.

There are two processes that allow firms to get bigger. The first is what Marx calls the "concentration of capital". This is a straightforward result of accumulation through which the units of capital grow over time. Consider, for instance, a capitalist with a rate of profit of 10 percent. After ten years, all other things remaining equal, they have grabbed enough surplus value to cover their total initial investment. If they saved all this surplus value they could now begin the same production process but on twice the scale as before. Concentration of capital tends to be a gradual process, taking place continuously over many years.

The "centralisation of capital" is a much faster process, and one that tends to leap forward in each economic crisis. In this process existing companies are drawn together into a single company, for instance through takeovers or mergers. The development of financial systems and the stock market can accelerate this process, as we shall see when we consider these topics. The centralisation of capital is an important feature of economic crises because surviving companies will often be able swallow up those that go bust at a fraction of their value.

Both processes, the concentration and centralisation of capital, promote more of the same. Big companies can consolidate different stages of the production process previously performed by different companies, get hold of raw materials at preferential rates, cut transport costs and make other savings. Because of their size they can afford to make the huge investments needed to acquire the most advanced machinery and technology. They can also seek markets on a far greater scale. For many giant firms the market for their commodities is not simply located within a single country, but may have a regional or even global scope. Large firms can also bring greater pressure to bear on governments by lobbying for special treatment, and often there is a "revolving door" between the boards of these companies and the corridors of state power. These advantages of scale can force the competitors of a giant firm to merge in order to survive.

This process can be seen at work in many sectors of the economy. In the pharmaceutical sector the four biggest companies are Johnson & Johnson, Pfizer, Bayer and GlaxoSmithKlein. Johnson & Johnson lists ten major mergers or acquisitions since the Second World War on its website. For the same period Pfizer lists five, Bayer ten, and GlaxoSmithKlein 16. The history of these giant companies is a saga of purchasing other companies to enter new markets, merging to grab more market share and invest on a biggest scale, and expanding geographically and taking advantage of crises to acquire less successful competitors.

While new, smaller companies are constantly being created, with many going bust and a few surviving, it is large firms that dominate the economy today. And often lurking behind seemingly small "footloose" companies are much bigger organisations. To take an extreme example, the Linux operating system, "open-source" computer software that competes with Microsoft's Windows, is often viewed as being developed by volunteers with a completely different ethos and business model to that in commercial software development. But almost all of those involved in its development were workers released by other computer giants such as Hewlett-Packard, Xerox and Sun, who sought to gain a competitive advantage over Microsoft.

Those few small companies that do find a niche and begin to break through either tend to become new giants or are bought up by existing ones.

As capitalism ages new problems emerge. The scale of corporations today makes it far harder for an economic crisis to restore the health of the system. We have already seen how the collapse of one firm can trigger a chain of collapses throughout the economy. The collapse of a large multinational, even an unprofitable one, can do this on a much bigger scale than the collapse of a small company. The danger is that such collapses turn a mild recession into an economic meltdown. For instance, WalMart, the biggest corporation in the world, has $160 billion in assets and makes $12 billion in profit each year. Its annual turnover is about the same as the GDP of Norway. The collapse of a giant such as this would create a huge hole in the economy, threatening to throw its two million employees out of work and dragging down scores of suppliers with it.

Throughout the 20th century, and especially in the post-war period, states have intervened time and again to protect big corporations through bail-outs or nationalisations. The temptation to do so grows as the units of capital grow, raising the stakes for the system. Politicians who may have preached the neoliberal dogma that there is no alternative to the market, claiming to hold the view that capitalism is a self-regulating system best left to its own devices, are in practice forced to attempt to rescue their system.

However, bailing companies out is no solution to the fundamental contradictions of the capitalist system. We have seen how crisis can restore some level of "health" to the economy. If states are too terrified to let large firms to go bust, then problems continue to accumulate for the future. Preventing a big crisis today can simply lead to an even bigger crisis tomorrow.

One final feature of ageing capitalism deserves comment. Large corporations do not simply represent huge concentrations of wealth and power. They also bring together huge concentrations of workers. In the US, the world's biggest economy, half of all workers are employed in enterprises with over 500 employees, and over two thirds in enterprises with over 100 employees. Contrary to much of the "common sense" on the left, which talks of the emergence of a "new economy" based on small, high tech companies, both these figures have increased in the past two decades. In Britain most workers are based in enterprises with over 250 employees. Similar figures hold for most advanced economies. The centralisation and concentration of capitalism potentially simplify the task facing those workers. They create a world ripe for socialism in which the key strategic goal is drawing together the workers in these fortresses of capital and taking control of the vast resources they command. The task of "planning", a much maligned but very necessary feature of a socialist economy, is simplified because multinationals already plan on a huge scale. The problem is to overcome the type of planning under capitalism: planning for private profit rather than democratic planning to meet social needs.

The distribution of surplus value

Until now I have assumed that all surplus value becomes profit for the capitalist who controls the production process. This is a useful abstraction if we wish to understand where profit originates and how it is pumped back into production through competitive accumulation. But in reality only a portion of the surplus value squeezed out of workers becomes profit. Other important uses of surplus value include rent, taxation and interest payments.

Rent is surplus value captured by landowners. Marx's theory of rent is developed in one of the most concrete and complex parts of *Capital*, and is presented towards the end of the third volume. I provide a basic summary of the theory in an appendix to this work.

Surplus value may find its way into the state's coffers through various means such as the direct taxation of profits. For instance, corporate profits were taxed at 28 percent for large companies in Britain in 2008, even if "creative accounting" allowed many capitalists to avoid this. But the state is not simply a drain on surplus value. It is also centrally important to the reproduction and accumulation of capital, just as many forms of labour are vital for capitalism even though they do not directly produce new surplus value. To see the state sector as in some sense "non-capitalist" or "outside capitalism" is to ignore the range of institutions and types of labour that capital requires to support the accumulation process.

Finally, in order to understand the development of capitalism and its crises, it is vital to understand the role of interest—and more generally the credit and financial system, which plays a central role in contemporary capitalism. This is our next task.

The world of finance

Earlier I described how money, a "universal equivalent", emerges historically, allowing goods to be exchanged and value to circulate through the economy. However, not every transaction requires the actual exchange of gold or even paper money issued by states and representing gold. Indeed, if every purchase was based on a capitalist handing over a pile of money, in whatever form, the business world as we know it could not function.

As capitalism develops, individual producers, connected together as suppliers and markets for each other's commodities, extend credit to each other. This leads to the creation of systems of "bills of exchange" and "credit notes", issued privately and passed between businesses. As they circulate, some of the credit and debt represented by these will cancel out, while traditional forms of money can, when payment is due, be used to settle what debts remain. This system of credit makes the circulation of capital far more rapid and efficient. Already in Marx's time the volume of this "credit money" being circulated outstripped the amount of paper money being used in England.

Of course such a system of credit money relies on the confidence that capitalists have in each other's businesses—and this in turn depends on the ability of capitalists to produce goods and sell them to someone at a healthy price. We have already seen that this is by no means automatic. Credit money can rapidly lose its value and debts are not always paid. Greater fluidity and efficiency come at a price.

The earliest bills of exchange represented specific goods being traded. The system of credit money is modified as banks emerge. Banks can replace the numerous forms of credit money issued by private producers with their own standardised banknotes, unrelated to any particular good or transaction. And they can guarantee the quality of money, at least insomuch as the bank remains solvent and capable of fulfilling its obligations. In the process banks also have to decide which capitalists are creditworthy and which are not.

Banks play a key role in creating money through expanding credit (a point overlooked by crude monetarist theories that claim the state can regulate the money supply). Typically banks hold a certain portion of their deposits as reserves—cash in their vaults or deposits with a central bank—and often the precise ratio is regulated by law. So in the US, where 10 percent of deposits must be held as reserves, for every $100 a bank receives in deposits it can lend out $90. If that $90 ends up in another bank account, that bank can in turn lend out $81, ensuring it keeps $9 in its reserves. As this process continues the initial deposit creates potential credit of $1,000. It appears as if money is simply created from thin air. But, as we shall see, this rests heavily on the confidence that capitalists have in the process of value creation in the wider economy.

Banks are a key component of the monetary system. But there are significant limitations to this private system of credit. As Geoffrey Ingham has pointed out:

Early private credit networks were unstable; they were only as strong as the networks of commerce in which they were embedded. Defaults on repayments broke the chains in the banking system's expansion of credit by causing bankruptcies and triggering recessions... Greater stability [was] achieved when the private banking networks were integrated with the public currency and sovereign debt of the most powerful and secure states.

This historic development laid the basis for the emergence of central banks such as the Bank of England or the Federal Reserve in the US, which drew together traditional monetary systems (such as those based on gold or tokens representing gold) with the growing system of private credit. Central banks are typically backed by the authority of the state, even when they are legally constituted as private institutions. By securing the system of credit, connecting it to the authority of the state and allowing banks to settle accounts with each other, central banks become the pivots around which national financial systems revolve. They guarantee the quality of money, decide which banks are creditworthy and issue the most universally accepted legal tender. These forms of money, for instance the notes issued by the Bank of England, generally become the form used for making small payments (although in Scotland, for example, banknotes issued by three large private banks are still widely used). Marx often assumes that that the money in circulation is convertible to gold. However, he also talks of "inconvertible paper money issued by the state and having compulsory circulation"—or "fiat money", whose role is legally enforced by governments.

In advanced capitalism only a relatively small amount of money circulates in the form of paper notes, let alone gold. Once capitalists begin depositing their money in banks (so loaning the money to the bank) they can make payments through the banking system instead. So money passes from the account of one company to that of another, or from the company's account to that of an employee as wages. Today even the day to day purchases made by workers are likely to be made with credit or debit cards, rather than physical coins or notes.

If banks settle accounts between businesses and central banks settle accounts between banks, how are accounts settled between different states with different currencies and banking systems? Huge imbalances can and do develop between states. Exchange rates between different countries fluctuate and become an area of speculation as currency traders bet on these changes. Global finance is, therefore, a very unstable and fluid system.

In practice, the most powerful states, and since the Second World War this meant the US in particular, tend to dominate this world financial system. From 1945 to 1971 the Bretton Woods Agreement saw the US dollar fixed in value against gold (and most of the world's gold was, at least at first, held by the US). This allowed the dollar to function as the universal equivalent on a world scale: other currencies were fixed against it. But the devaluation of the dollar in 1971, as other economies began to challenge the US's dominance and the US government ran up a huge deficit as it pumped money into the Vietnam War, severed this link—just as the earlier "gold standard" based on the strength of sterling had collapsed in the 1920s. The system of floating exchange rates that succeeded it came under pressure in turn due to further shifts in the balance of economic power.

Financial disorders are not simply a peripheral feature of capitalism. Credit plays a central role in the most basic processes of capital accumulation and it lies at the core of Marx's account of the system. Capitalists, as we have seen, compete by investing some of their surplus value to accumulate more capital. What happens when capitalists do not have an immediate outlet for their profits or if they need to invest but have not yet saved sufficient money to do so? Banks and other financial institutions provide a means of financing investment for some capitalists, while providing an immediate outlet for the profits of others. They draw money together in all its different forms and make it available as a form of capital.

For example, a capitalist might save money in a bank account hoping to invest it later. The bank can then lend it to a different capitalist who wants to invest now. And in general banks will gather money from whatever source they can, including the savings of workers, the rent of landowners and so on, in order to harness it all as capital. This directly exposes workers as well as capitalists to the disorders associated with finance.

Lending and borrowing give an added impetus to accumulation, as well as the centralisation of capital, but are also a source of increased instability. If there is a sudden fall in profit rates or a loss of faith in the market, panic can spread rapidly through the system as debts are called in. Finance accelerates all the processes associated with capitalism—making it both more dynamic *and* more destructive and crisis-prone. Capital can flow much faster in and out of different areas of the economy when it exists as money than when it exists as machinery or the commodities produced by a factory. Credit is a powerful lubricant for the system, for better and for worse. As Marx puts it, "Banking and credit thus become the most potent means of driving capitalist production beyond its own limits—and one of the most effective vehicles of crises and swindle."

Marx notes another feature of this credit system. The money lent by financial institutions such as banks is a special kind of capital, which he calls "interest bearing capital". When it is lent to a capitalist, interest bearing capital is an instance of capital itself becoming a commodity. We know that commodities must have a use-value and an exchange-value. The use-value of interest bearing capital is simply its ability to "expand", to increase in value. But its exchange-value—the interest it earns—is, in Marx's words, "irrational". It bears no direct relationship to the process of production. It makes no sense to try to measure the labour time to create the purest representation of value (money) while it is in the process of expansion.

There is, therefore, no "natural" rate of interest. Unlike the rate of profit, the rate of interest cannot be understood simply through an appeal to underlying laws of motion of capitalist production. Interest rates are shaped by the supply of and demand for interest bearing capital, and the competitive relationship between those capitalists specialising in lending money and those who need to borrow it. (Often the distinction between these two groups is blurred because, in practice, large numbers of "industrial capitalists" are also involved in finance, for example car manufacturers who extend credit to buyers.) The rate of interest will tend, therefore, to change through the course of the business cycle as the demand for interest bearing capital fluctuates. The movement of interest rates can shape the course of both the boom and the bust. Finance, therefore, coordinates capital on a national and global level, drawing together disparate and uneven patterns of accumulation into a single rhythm. This is why so many of the crises of contemporary capitalism appear in the form of financial crises.

Often for the capitalist what is important is not just profit but what Marx calls "profit of enterprise", which he defines as profit minus interest payments. This is obviously the case when the capitalist is operating with borrowed capital that must be repaid with interest. But even when capitalists are operating with their own capital they are interested in what they earn over and above the going rate of interest. This is because interest increasingly appears as the money that capital automatically earns, for instance while sitting in a bank account. This is an extreme form of commodity fetishism that obscures the real source of capital's self-expansion: the exploitation of living labour.

Fictitious capital

OFTEN credit is advanced against a *potential* future value. For example, a capitalist who intends to print books might issue £1 million of bonds—pieces of paper entitling the purchaser to a share of the income produced by the capitalist. Investors can then buy these bonds. Imagine that the capitalist buys a printing press using the £1 million raised and produces the books. After the books are sold the capitalist repays the investors (plus any additional payments agreed between them). Anything left over is the profit of the capitalist.

Now, in this example, the capitalist has used the £1 million raised as capital in its "real" sense: it was invested to generate surplus value. But the bond investors simply hold pieces of paper, the bonds they have purchased, entitling them to a share of the value. These bonds are not capital in the sense in which we have encountered it so far. The capital does not exist twice—once for the capitalist and once for the investor. However, our investor might then trade these bonds; indeed, a whole market in similar bonds might exist, and they might shift in value according to their supply and demand or the imagined prospects for future earnings. This is a market in "fictitious capital".

Marx used this term to describe a whole range of claims on value that could then be traded. In general, a claim on property of a certain value is "capitalised"—it is turned into a stream of income typically based on the going rate of interest. Marx writes:

The formation of a fictitious capital is called capitalisation. Every periodic income is capitalised by calculating it on the basis of the average rate of interest, as an income which would be realised by a capital loaned at this rate of interest.

One of the most important markets for fictitious capital is the stock market. Companies floated on the stock exchange issue shares in order to raise money. These shares then form fictitious capital that can be bought and sold by traders. The prices of shares are not directly linked to the production of values but instead fluctuate according to their own laws. The values of shares may soar way above the value they initially represented, and may come crashing down again as the stock market collapses.

For instance, during the late 1990s in the US the "dot-com" bubble saw a huge increase in the share prices of high technology and internet based firms, many of which had never generated a profit. The ratio of stock prices to profits rose to at least twice its historic average before the bubble suddenly burst in 2001.

But fictitious capital is generally, however tenuously, connected to productive capital, even if it follows different laws. For instance, those who hold shares might hope to earn dividends that the company pays out to shareholders. In other words, shares are a claim on surplus value and thus participate in the redistribution of surplus value I discussed earlier. But shares are titles of ownership on real capital, rather than capital itself. If I buy shares in a company and they later become worthless in a crash, the company still has the value I paid, which it may have invested and used as real capital. No real capital has been destroyed by the stock market crash. Value has merely been transferred from me to the company.

Of course, a stock market crash can still have "real" consequences. For instance, firms that specialise in trading shares could cancel the purchase of office buildings or throw employees out of work, cutting their consumption. And if a firm's shares collapse in value it can destroy confidence in that firm, making it hard for its owners to raise funds. Finally, if a worker's pension fund or savings are invested in shares that decline in value, the effects on the worker can be very real. But this is still not the destruction of value; it is the transfer of money from the pension fund (and ultimately the wages of the worker) to the person who sold the shares to the fund.

Along with the growth of the credit system comes the growth of any number of new forms of fictitious capital—mortgages representing a claim on future rent, government bonds representing claims on future tax revenue, "futures" representing claims on the future values of commodities such as grain or oil, and so on. The trade in this fictitious capital does not in itself create new value or expand production, but it gives new fluidity to capitalism, as markets seem to spring up overnight and vast quantities of money are mobilised for speculative purposes. It can fixate and fascinate the financial commentators as it seems to, as if by magic, generate untold riches, at least until the market comes crashing down.

Unravelling Capitalism

A second look at crisis

THE development of a complex financial system and markets in fictitious capital modifies our understanding of economic crises. For one thing, entirely new kinds of banking or stock market crises are now possible which have a complicated and indirect relationship to the underlying "real" economy. But it is also possible for finance to exacerbate and shape the booms and busts that are intrinsic to capitalism.

Marx traces the general pattern in *Capital*. As a new boom gets under way there will be a large quantity of money capital with very few outlets. For the reasons set out earlier, the interest rate will therefore tend to be low. At first capitalists may have their own unused reserves of cash left over from the preceding recession that may fund their investment. But as the boom develops they will be increasingly dependent on external sources of finance. Demand for money capital grows and interest rates begin to rise.

As the boom in accumulation is beginning to create problems for the "real" economy, it also begins to create many kinds of speculative activity. New forms of fictitious capital are created; stock market prices can soar ahead of the real profits generated by companies. Credit, in all its forms, expands. Banks look for ever riskier lending opportunities as the number of established borrowers dries up. Falling profit rates can make speculation seem far more lucrative than investing in the "real" economy. Asset prices can shoot up, forming speculative "bubbles" that can burst just as rapidly, sending investors into a panic and destroying confidence in the economy as a whole.

As the crisis breaks, the problems in the underlying economy begin to assert themselves. Credit, as we have seen, helps to drive capitalism beyond its limits. If capitalism is like a balloon with the various firms painted on its surface, credit is like the air pumped inside it. As the balloon expands the surface tension grows. Chains of debt bind the companies and banks together ever more tightly. And a pin prick at any point can burst the whole balloon. Extending credit ultimately relies on the health of the "real" economy, where goods are produced and services provided, and credit cannot lose touch entirely with the production of new value. If you want to keep pumping air into the balloon, eventually you need a balloon made from a greater amount of rubber.

As the economic crisis begins to break, investors start to panic about the quality of credit they have extended and look to return to the security of money. Existing debts must be settled and demand for money—gold or the high quality money issued by central banks—grows. Interest rates shoot up. The developing financial and monetary crisis now accelerates the underlying contradictions in the economy. It also spreads the crisis as chains of borrowing and lending that helped fuel the preceding boom are severed.

An article in the *Financial Times* in autumn 2008, written as the British economy tipped towards recession, captures the importance of this rush to the security of money and the calling in of debts:

> For the first time since the last recession of the early 1990s the management of working capital—the amount of cash that a company needs to operate on

a day to day basis—has shot to the forefront of executives' minds... The squeeze on working capital is tightening as the cost of supplies rises and incoming cash declines... Retailers, such as Asda and Tesco, have been trying to extend payment terms to their suppliers... Earlier in the year Premier Foods— owner of the Hovis bread and Campbell's soup brands—boosted its cash reserves by £100 million after selling a chunk of payments due from debtors to a specialist firm...

Working capital is often expressed in terms of the number of days worth of sales tied up in working capital, or "days working capital"... Brian Shanahan, director at [consultancy firm] REL, says, "The funding models that everyone's been running have radically changed in the last 12 months so if you are a net borrower this suggests the squeeze is on. Days working capital is edging up, profits are edging down and the banks are getting tougher. You are almost being caught from both angles."

A second transformation in the nature of capitalist crisis occurs with the modern system of finance. Once "commodity money" such as gold or silver was replaced by convertible paper and credit money it could, in periods of expansion and growth, be issued in far greater quantities than the gold it represented. Indeed this was necessary in order to speed circulation of capital on an ever expanding scale. But in a crisis there is a rush towards the most secure forms of money. Those who have extended credit, in whatever form, seek money as payment. Those with money will, if the money is convertible into gold, seek gold.

Governments and central banks that issued money could be forced to suspend its convertibility and the paper money could, therefore, fall in value with, for example, each £10 note representing less and less value (in terms of the labour time it commands). Once the connection between gold and money issued by central banks is completely severed, as has happened in most modern economies, new money can be issued with great flexibility, but now the state's authority is the only thing securing its value. So as economic crisis broke out in 2008 the value of the dollar rose as fearful investors poured their money into what they perceived as the most secure currency, backed by the largest and most powerful state.

In the course of accumulation the amount of value circulated expands. Money and credit must expand accordingly. But if this expansion proceeds faster than the expansion of value in the economy, inflation—a sustained rise in the prices of commodities—becomes a possibility. Inflation is not an automatic response to the expansion of money and credit. For example, it is perfectly possible for production to expand or for money to be hoarded. What happens in the wider economy plays a role in determining the rate of inflation.

We have already seen that as productivity grows the rate of profit tends to decline and the value embodied in particular commodities falls. Capitalists can try to offset this by maintaining or raising the prices of the goods they produce. The temptation to do this will be greatest when the rate of accumulation is still high, driving up overall demand, but the rate of profit is falling. The tendency is greatly exacerbated with the development of monopolies, which can arbitrarily raise prices with little fear of competitors undercutting them. While in early economic crises prices usually fell (known as deflation), in the second half of the 20th century larger companies were increasingly able to hold prices high during a crisis, spreading the pain elsewhere in the system. States may also step in to purchase unsold goods and increase overall demand in the economy to try to prevent economic crisis. Hyper-inflation also becomes a possibility if states simply decide to print more and more money, for instance to bail out firms, destroying its value.

While it is still true that the value of commodities—the labour time embodied within them—tends to fall during the process of accumulation, their price in money terms can simultaneously rise. This can, for a time, offset the tendency of the rate of profit to fall. But this will impact on the subsequent period of production, as capitalists now have to pay more to purchase the goods they need in production and workers have to pay more to purchase the things they consume. Prices cannot return to their old levels without cutting profit rates even more sharply, and a new wave of price rises will tend to follow to maintain high profit rates. So inflation in one cycle tends to encourage more inflation. Ultimately only the devaluation of capital through crisis can resolve these problems. Spiralling inflation simply postpones the crisis, and generally exacerbates underlying imbalances and contradictions in the economy. It tends to spread the impact of the crisis across society as a whole. For instance, it reduces the value of debts and diminishes the value of savings, eradicating distinctions between more and less prudent businesses. Inflation can also increase pressure on workers to fight to maintain their "real" wage as they find their pay packet can purchase less and less.

The decline in the value of a currency can also disturb the international financial structure as currencies shift in value relative to each other, placing pressure on exchange rates and weakening the position of some states in the wider financial hierarchy—although a weaker currency can also boost exports by making them cheaper for overseas buyers.

Most economies have experienced some inflation for most of the 20th century, and a low level of inflation is consistent with a growing economy. An economic crisis might be deflationary—as was the great depression of the 1930s. Then prices fell as firms desperately sought to sell their goods in collapsing markets and credit dried up as banks failed. But a crisis might also see "stagflation", a combination of inflation with economic stagnation, as happened in the 1970s. States and central bankers, through their monetary policies, their intervention in markets and so on, have some power to affect how the crisis manifests itself. But they cannot remove the underlying contradictions that lead capitalism, again and again, into crisis.

Phenomena such as inflation, fictitious capital and the development of crises are fiendishly complicated even when considered in the context of a particular national economy. These complexities are multiplied once the world system made up of competing national economies is taken into account. Marx's theory contains the seeds of an understanding of such phenomena. But none of these problems are by any means "solved" and much work remains for Marxists attempting to get to grips with the contemporary capitalist system. Some of the further reading suggested at the end of this book grapples with these problems, which are merely touched upon here.

Prices and the general rate of profit

A s we have already noted, in the third volume of
Capital Marx develops a more concrete picture of
capitalism, building on the work of the preceding volumes. It is here that he outlines his ideas on credit and
rent, and his approach to economic crisis. But as
Marx moves towards a more concrete picture of the
system he is also forced to drop many of the simplify-
ing assumptions he had made in order to understand
capitalism's basic laws of motion. One consequence is
that the relationship between prices and values is sub-
stantially altered.

Now Marx shows how prices of commodities *sys-
tematically* deviate from their values—rather than
simply oscillating around values due to fluctuations in
supply and demand, as he assumes in the first two volumes of *Capital*. Although this process is somewhat
complex, to really comprehend Marx's political economy it is necessary to contend with it. In this chapter I
merely outline Marx's argument. I comment on the intense and ongoing controversy around these issues that
has become known as the "transformation problem" in
an appendix to this book.

First let us recap what Marx writes about value in the
first volume of *Capital*. For Marx the value of a commodity reflects the amount of living labour expended by
workers in its creation, plus the amount of dead labour
transferred to it during the production process. The
value can be measured as a sum of money reflecting the

socially necessary labour time required to produce the commodity under normal conditions with the average prevalent skill and intensity. The capitalist has to purchase the dead labour and makes no profit from this. The source of profit is living labour. The capitalist receives a day's labour but only has to pay enough, in the form of a day's wages, for the reproduction of the labour power of the worker. The gap between this value of labour power and the new value created by the workers provides surplus value for the capitalist, and this is the basis for profit. We also defined the rate of profit as the ratio of surplus value to the total capital advanced in wages and inputs of dead labour. It appears to the capitalist that their profit is based on *both* living and dead labour, even though this is not the case. Finally, we saw that, all else remaining equal, the rate of profit falls as the organic composition of capital rises.

This analysis allows Marx to discover the origin of surplus value in the exploitation at the heart of the capitalist production process. But when Marx begins to consider a more concrete capitalist economy, with many different coexisting branches, a problem emerges.

Different branches of the economy have different organic compositions of capital, unless they happen to coincide by chance. This implies that each branch should also have a different rate of profit. But in capitalism as it actually exists, profit rates tend to equalise across economies, tending towards a "general rate of profit". How does this general rate of profit come about?

Capitalists will naturally try to maximise their profitability by investing in those branches with the highest profit rate. Marx argues that capital can flow between branches of the economy, from those with high organic compositions of capital (and hence low rates of profit) to those with low organic compositions (and high rates of profit). Commodities in branches with a high rate of profit will be produced in greater quantities, lowering their prices, while those in branches with a low rate of profit will become scarce and their prices will rise. Over time these changes in price will tend to equalise profit rates between branches. This process is the "transformation" of values into what Marx calls "prices of production".

Some commentators have argued that in this analysis Marx is ditching his theory of value (and have either praised or criticised him for doing so, depending on their personal predilection). In fact, prices of production are simply a *more complex expression of value*. The surplus value pumped out of living labour is reallocated to different capitalists in such a way as to form a general rate of profit. In order for the rate of profit to be the same in each branch of the economy the capitalists would each have to receive the same amount of surplus value per pound of capital they invest. It would really appear as if *all* their capital was generating surplus value, rather than just the living labour.

In other words, their total input costs, their "costs of production" in Marx's phrase, would be marked up according to the general rate of profit. It appears as if the capitalist simply receives from society a share of total surplus value reflecting their investment. So, if the total cost of printing a newspaper to the capitalist in the print industry was £1 in wages, machinery, raw material, etc, and the general rate of profit was 10 percent, the price of a newspaper would be £1.10p.

To show how this works using some simple mathematics, consider an economy consisting of just two branches with different organic compositions of capital. Capitalists in the first branch invest £40 constant capital, £60 variable capital; in the second they invest £60

constant capital, £40 variable capital. We will imagine
that half the time workers are covering the value of their
wage and half the time they are generating surplus value
(so that the surplus value for each capitalist is equal to
the variable capital they invest).

Values

	Branch 1	Branch 2
c	£40	£60
v	£60	£40
s	£60	£40
Organic Composition of Capital [c / v]	$40/60 = 2/3$	$60/40 = 1 1/2$
Rate of profit [s / (c + v)]	$60/100 = 60\%$	$40/100 = 40\%$
Value of output [s + c + v]	£160	£140

c = constant capital; v = variable capital; s = surplus value

In this example, the branch with the highest organic
composition (branch two) has a lower rate of profit.
Capital would flow between branches, changing the
prices of the output of each. Eventually the rate of profit
would tend towards the general rate, which is simply
the ratio of total surplus value to total capital invested:

General rate of profit
$$= \text{Total s / (total c + total v)}$$
$$= 100/(100 + 100)$$
$$= 1/2 = 50\%$$

Now if both types of capitalist invest a total of £100
in capital, they would both get a return of £50 profit (ie
a 50% rate of profit). So:

Transforming values to prices

	Branch 1	Branch 2
c	£40	£60
v	£60	£40
s	£60	£40
Organic Composition of Capital [c / v]	$40/60 = 2/3$	$60/40 = 1\ 1/2$
Profit rate	50%	50%
Profit	£50	£50
Cost of production [c + v]	£100	£100
Price of production	£150	£150

This is a very simple example. In reality the capital actually *consumed* in the period being considered would not be the same as the total capital *invested* because some of the constant capital would be fixed capital, used again and again. This means that two different values of constant capital would be involved in the calculation of the price of the output. The capital consumed would give the cost of production, while the profit would be calculated on the *total* capital advanced by the capitalist.

These subtleties aside, one thing should be clear from the example. The *total amount of surplus value* in the first table (£100) is the same as the *total amount of profit* in the second. Similarly the total value of the output is the same as the total price of the output. This is an important point. According to Marx's analysis, prices of production are a complex form assumed by value. It does not alter the fact that exploitation forms the heart of capitalism. The total amount of value created in the economy is always the same as the total price of all the goods and services produced. The total profit of the different capitalists is always the same as the total surplus value pumped out of the working class. All that has happened is that some of the surplus value has been redistributed among the capitalists so that each claims a share in proportion to the capital they invest.

Marx added in his analysis that, once this redistribution is taken into account, certain groups of capitalists who do not produce surplus value might also grab their share (aside from the other claims on surplus value we considered earlier, such as rent and interest). In particular those involved in money dealing (bookkeeping and so on) or merchants, who perform roles that could equally be performed by productive capitalists themselves, can expect to acquire profit at the general rate based on their investment.

Finally, Marx is not attempting to develop an equilibrium theory giving stable prices for commodities. Perfect equilibrium, with every sector of the economy receiving exactly the general rate of profit and prices of production all settled at the "correct" levels, never comes about. Market prices now oscillate about prices of production (rather than values); capital attempts to flow between sectors, but cannot do so instantly and often faces impediments—not least the fact that capital is embedded in particular factories and machinery. The dynamism of the economy, the process of accumulation, competition, the rising organic composition of capital and its regular devaluation all act to disturb the "equilibrium" before it is ever fully established.

Politics of the crisis

"A recession—great!" "A slump—wonderful!" This is the caricature of the socialist response to economic crisis. Capitalism starts to fall apart, workers realise that socialism is the answer and the revolution gets under way. Red flags are unfurled and barricades built. Of course, nothing could be further from the truth. There is no direct correlation between economic patterns and class struggle or political consciousness. A deep depression, causing poverty and mass unemployment, can just as easily demoralise workers and throw them onto the defensive as send them out to the barricades.

Marx and Engels had their first direct experience of revolutionary struggle during the wave of revolt that swept Europe in 1848. This followed hot on the heels of an economic crisis in 1847, though this was merely the immediate trigger for the revolts, which had other underlying political causes. After the revolutionary wave a new period of capitalist prosperity began, which lasted for more than two decades. The Russian revolutionary Leon Trotsky, commenting on this in 1921, noted:

> Engels wrote that while the crisis of 1847 was the mother of revolutions, the boom of 1849-51 was the mother of triumphant counter-revolution. It would, however, be very one-sided and utterly false to interpret these judgements in the sense that a crisis invariably engenders revolutionary action while a boom, on the contrary, pacifies the working class.

Trotsky contrasted Marx and Engels's experience with the period immediately after the 1905 Revolution in Russia:

> The 1905 Revolution was defeated. The workers bore great sacrifices. In 1906 and 1907 the last revolutionary flare-ups occurred and by the autumn of 1907 a great world crisis broke out... Throughout 1907 and 1908 and 1909 the most terrible crisis reigned in Russia too. It killed the movement completely, because the workers had suffered so greatly during the struggle that the depression could act only to dishearten them.

The struggle in Russia, culminating in the 1917 Revolution, only recovered when the economy began to pick up and workers became more confident. These examples alone show that the exact relationship between economics and politics is complex, and that vague general principles will not suffice.

Another myth is that the utter impoverishment of workers is a necessary precondition for socialist revolution. Again, there is no correlation between the degree of suffering of workers and their willingness to fight. It is not true that the degree to which much of Africa has been hurled back economically in recent decades has led to it automatically becoming a hotbed of revolution, though there have been heroic struggles in *certain countries* at *certain times*. Some of the recent high points of struggle have taken place in relatively wealthy areas of the world—Venezuela and Argentina (two of the richer Latin American economies), South Africa and Egypt (wealthy by African standards), and Greece—as well as much poorer countries such as Bolivia or Nepal.

Some kind of crisis is a factor in creating a revolutionary situation, although this can equally be a political crisis, for instance one produced by a disastrous war. But crisis does not automatically lead to a revolution. As Lenin put it, a revolution is possible "only when the 'lower classes' do not want to live in the old way and the 'upper classes' cannot carry on in the old way". Crisis can help create such a situation because workers can suddenly question whether they will lead a better life or enjoy a certain level of wages to which they have become accustomed. This in turn can, in the right circumstances, stimulate political debate and struggle as old certainties dissolve. Crisis can also crack apart the confidence and coherence of the ruling class, preventing them from ruling "in the old way".

Our rulers might have a common interest in exploiting workers, but the capitalist class are also run through with internal divisions as they engage in competitive accumulation. An economic crisis can sharpen the struggle between capitalists and workers as the capitalists struggle to squeeze more wealth out of their employees. It can also exacerbate tensions in the ruling class as they fight among themselves over the surplus value remaining, attempt to shift the burden onto each other and put forward different policies to try to claw their way out of the crisis. All this creates cracks at the top of society and provides space for those at the bottom to put forward their own demands and their own solutions. The very dynamism of the capitalist system leads to political instability and, often quite unexpectedly, explosions of popular anger.

Part 3

The changing system

The classical period

MARX'S world was shaped by two revolutions. The great French Revolution of 1789 had broken the political rule of the old feudal aristocracy far more decisively than the English Revolution a century earlier or the Dutch Revolt before that. The emerging capitalist ruling class could only destroy the power of the old rulers by harnessing the power of the mass of people for a moment behind slogans such as "Liberty, Equality, Fraternity". As capitalism strengthened its grip on society it became clear that liberty meant the liberty of workers to sell their labour to capitalists, equality meant meeting as "equals" in the marketplace and fraternity meant the brotherhood of the new rulers as they exploited the growing mass of workers.

Over subsequent decades a new antagonism came to the fore, that between workers and capitalists. Future "bourgeois revolutions" would be carried out from the top down by sections of the old elite, who had no desire to risk violent revolutionary change that might see workers settle scores with their new exploiters along with the feudal ruling class.

The second great revolution shaping Marx's world was the industrial revolution centred on Britain, which gathered pace towards the end of the 18th century. Already Britain had experienced a bourgeois revolution of its own. Already the old feudal way of doing things had begun breaking down. Traditional agriculture was transformed into capitalist farming based on wage labour; merchants were increasing the levels of trade and speeding the establishment of towns as centres of commerce and handicraft production. Where wool merchants had once delivered wool to peasant families to be spun and then collected the thread to sell on to weavers, they now drew labour together directly in "manufactures" and oversaw this process from beginning to end. In such manufactures they could establish a "division of labour", dividing complex tasks into several simple ones to accelerate the production process. As these kinds of labour became more central to society labourers were increasingly paid in money. The market received another boost as labourers had to pay for their basic needs, rather than producing the bulk of their own means of subsistence in their own household. Society as a whole was being drawn into a web of market relations.

It was only a small step from the manufactures of the 17th and early 18th centuries to the factories of the industrial revolution. Now individual tasks, already subject to the division of labour, could be performed by machinery operated by workers. The development of water power and later steam power drove the productivity of labour forward. The world of industrial capitalism was born. As we have seen, capitalism is capable of rapid expansion and accumulation. It is the most dynamic system ever seen. Marx and Engels's words in the *Communist Manifesto* capture this:

> The bourgeoisie…has accomplished wonders far surpassing Egyptian pyramids, Roman aqueducts and Gothic cathedrals; it has conducted expeditions that put in the shade all former exoduses of nations and crusades… The need of a constantly expanding market for its products chases the bourgeoisie over the

entire surface of the globe. It must nestle everywhere, settle everywhere, establish connections everywhere...

The bourgeoisie, during its rule of scarce 100 years, has created more massive and more colossal productive forces than have all preceding generations together. Subjection of nature's forces to man, machinery, application of chemistry to industry and agriculture, steam navigation, railways, electric telegraphs, clearing of whole continents for cultivation, canalisation of rivers, whole populations conjured out of the ground—what earlier century had even a presentiment that such productive forces slumbered in the lap of social labour?

The classical capitalism of Marx's day already contained the seeds of its own transformation. As the passages quoted above make clear, capitalism is a global system. The world is, potentially, its market. The dynamism of the system allows it to settle everywhere and nestle everywhere. But it is also an uneven system. It develops with different speeds in different areas of the globe. It broke through first in Britain, the Low Countries, France and a few other areas of Europe and North America—later it spread across the Earth's surface. But this did not simply replicate the development of British or French capitalism. As capitalism developed it changed.

The second factor involved in the transformation of capitalism, along with its global spread, is the state. A capitalist economy requires a capitalist state. This is not necessarily a state directly run by capitalists themselves. Indeed, as the interests of different groups of capitalists clash, this might not be the best solution for the capitalist class as a whole. But it must be a state that is run in the interests of capital. It must ensure the functioning of markets, repress workers if they get out of hand, protect trade networks and so on. The state's monopoly of organised violence, for instance its control over armies, also makes it the perfect weapon for the forcible expansion of capitalism into territories where the new system has not yet broken through.

So the uneven spread and development of capitalism, and the centralised violence of the capitalist state came together to allow countries such as Britain and France to seize the first colonies—often in areas of the world that had been far more advanced just a few centuries earlier. This gave a further impetus to the early capitalist powers as they made use of the resources they plundered and the people they conquered.

Once this process of capitalist development and globalisation unfolds—once much of the world has been drawn into the capitalist system, either by independently developing its economy, by being conquered or by being pulled into the sphere of influence of one of the great powers—capitalism enters a new stage.

The birth of imperialism

Towards the end of the 19th century a new form of capitalism took shape. The centralisation and concentration of capital, accelerated by the growth of finance, led to the creation of vast corporations, trusts and cartels, monopolies and multinationals. Increasingly, the interests of a particular state were identified with the interests of the capitalists based there. And, as the units of capital grew in size, their own national market was no longer sufficient. Raw materials were required from across the globe, workers in many countries could be exploited and any population became a potential market for goods and services. So particular states and the corporations intertwined with them began to clash on the world stage.

But capitalism was, and still is, a system of "uneven and combined development", as the Russian Marxist Leon Trotsky put it. Those states that lag behind (a product of the unevenness of the system) feel compelled to introduce the most modern forms of industry, skipping intermediate stages of development. This means that different patterns of labour, forms of industry and technology are combined, drawn together in a particular context. So Russia before the 1917 Revolution was one of the most backward areas of Europe. Most people still lived on the land; those in the cities were first generation workers, usually illiterate and still bound by a thousand connections to the old agricultural system. Yet the Russian city of St Petersburg housed the biggest factory in the world—the giant Putilov steel works. Today if you fly into Hyderabad airport in India, you will see the slums of the city from one window of the aeroplane and the enormous shining complex known as "Cyber Towers", housing some of the world's biggest computing giants, from another. Elements of advanced capitalism can jostle with antiquated forms of agriculture, vast accumulations of wealth alongside obscene poverty.

The uneven and combined development of capitalism leads to conflict. While some countries struggle to break through at all, others manage to develop, sometimes very rapidly, and clash with established capitalist powers. This process sets the scene for imperialist rivalry as competition on a world scale takes the form of a struggle between states operating in the interest of rival groups of capitalists.

Imperialism is not simply the domination of colonies by the great powers—it involves clashes between the great powers themselves as they seek to redivide the globe at the expense of their rivals. So the rapid development of Germany late in the 19th century brought it into conflict with existing powers such as France and Britain, leading to the First and Second World Wars.

Once the imperialist system was established it provided a further drive to develop capitalism. Those nations that did not make the breakthrough faced domination by those that had already done so. This gave an even greater impetus for accumulation and for states to develop military machines to defend their capitalists' interests and threaten their rivals. Indeed, during the First World War states intervened in the economy in unprecedented ways, revealing a tendency for private capitalism, the state and the military to fuse together into a "state capitalist" block to compete with rival "state capitalisms". Although this was a short-lived affair—most states subsequently scaled back such intervention in the economy after the war had ended—it was to prefigure important developments in the next period.

The slump and state capitalism

THE period of classical capitalism and the growth of imperialism saw the expansion of world trade and economic output. But, as we have seen, the growth of capitalist productivity through accumulation puts pressure on profit rates and threatens the system's continued expansion. This had already begun to take its toll by the 1920s. According to some estimates profit rates fell by about 40 percent from 1880 to 1920 in the US. But crisis did not break out at once. Instead vast areas of unproductive expenditure sprang up: these included the luxury consumption of the rich, a huge expansion of lending and borrowing, and the growth of stock markets and other markets for fictitious capital. These contributed to continued optimism and even speculative frenzy. However, by 1929 unemployment was already rising in Europe and manufacturing had been in decline in both the US and Europe for some time.

The underlying problems became more obvious in October 1929 with the great stock market crash on Wall Street. The economic problems spread rapidly through the financial system as debts were called in, banks started to fail and those that remained raised interest rates in the face of growing demand for "good" money. The greatest slump in world history was under way— and the process of "creative destruction" that had previously restored the system to health seemed ineffective as unemployment grew and economies stagnated.

Eventually each of the great powers turned to some form of the "state capitalism" foreshadowed by the First World War. In the US the New Deal sought to give limited state backing to the private economy and to boost demand—and for a time this led to some recovery until 1937, when the US tipped back into recession. Ultimately it was only with the mobilisation for war, involving a far more dramatic level of intervention, which pulled the US out of the slump.

In Nazi Germany, as in the US, major capitalist firms were left intact. But under Hitler their investment decisions were subordinated to the drive to rearm and prepare for war, even when such investment was not particularly profitable. The state stepped in to organise investment and finance. While in France and Britain the level of state involvement was limited, late developing powers such as Japan rushed to follow the German example.

The Soviet Union saw state capitalism carried to its logical conclusion. By the time of the Wall Street Crash the gains of the 1917 Russian Revolution had already been reversed under the rule of Joseph Stalin. The Russian Revolution had been premised on the spread of workers' power across Europe. Its leaders, in particular Lenin and Trotsky, took it for granted that the prerequisites for socialism—highly developed means of production and a mass working class—did not exist on a sufficient scale in Russia itself. International revolution was required. For a period after the First World War it appeared as if revolution might spread to any number of European powers but by the late 1920s the revolutionary tide had ebbed. This paved the way for the rise of Stalin, who argued for "socialism in one country" rather than international revolution.

As Stalin wiped out the remnants of workers' control and democracy he began developing "state capitalism in

Unravelling Capitalism

one country". A tightly controlled state bureaucracy governed every major area of the economy. Human needs were subordinated to the need to accumulate and compete militarily with the other great powers, mirroring what was taking place in the "free market" economies elsewhere. In backward Russia the rush to accumulate took on a particularly savage form. Stalin argued in 1931, "We are 50 or 100 years behind the advanced countries. We must make good this lag in ten years. Either we do this or they crush us." Imperialist rivalry with other countries, rather than spreading the revolution, became the order of the day. In other words, imperialist competition between states enforced accumulation and exploitation in Russian state capitalism—just as free market competition had traditionally forced private capitalists to function as capitalists. The whole economy functioned like one giant factory, in competition with other giant factories.

The result of these developments was a world of state capitalisms—each with differing blends of "free market" and state control. World trade declined, falling sharply in the early 1930s and only much later recovering to the levels of the early 1920s.

By 1939 the imperialist tension produced by the uneven growth of capitalism, and the high levels of arms spending and militarisation of the 1930s, sharpened into war. Ultimately it was the destruction of capital in the Second World War, combined with arms spending and the forcible reorganisation of capitalist production by the state, that ended the great slump and prepared the way for the long boom that followed the war. The capitalism that emerged from the war was dramatically different from the system that existed in the 1920s. State involvement in the economy peaked during the war but never fell back to anything like its old levels.

The long boom

THE period following the Second World War saw the greatest sustained boom in history. It was a "golden age" for capitalism. This is often put down to the triumph of "Keynesian" economic theory, state planning or some compromise between capital and labour. In fact the "clearing out" and reorganisation of capital that accompanied slump and war paved the way for the boom. But to understand why the boom lasted until the mid-1970s we have to understand something more about the nature of inter-imperialist rivalry in this period.

The US and the Soviet Union emerged from the war as the world's great superpowers, with the US considerably larger than its rival and able to exert its influence over a far greater geographical area. Both spent massively on arms, not least through building up stockpiles of nuclear weapons. This arms spending, along with that of the key military powers in Nato and the Soviet dominated Warsaw Pact, helped to stabilise the capitalist system as a whole. Mike Kidron, who produced a series of pathbreaking essays on this topic, wrote:

> In so far as capital is taxed to sustain expenditure on arms it is deprived of resources that might otherwise go on further investment; in so far as expenditure on arms is expenditure on a fast wasting end product it constitutes a net addition to the market for consumer or "end" goods. Since one obvious result of such expenditure is full employment, and one result of full

employment is rates of growth amongst the highest ever, the dampening effect of such taxation is not readily apparent. But it is not absent. Were capital left alone to invest its entire pre-tax profit, the state creating demand as and when necessary, growth rates would be very much higher. Finally, since arms are a "luxury" in a sense that they are used neither as instruments of production nor as means of subsistence, in the production of other commodities, their production has no effect on profit rates overall.

The first part of the argument is straightforward—weapons production is a drain on the surplus value extracted by capitalists. They are taxed and the government takes their tax revenue and pumps it into weapons production. This can slow the level of investment by those capitalists, reducing the tendency for the organic composition of capital to rise and thus the decline in profit rates. The second part of the argument is that weapons spending is like the "luxury" spending of the rich. While wage goods and means of production feed back into capitalist production—forming the value of variable and constant capital respectively—the luxury goods consumed by capitalists do not play this role. They form a "leak" out of the capitalist system. Weapons are either stockpiled in arsenals or used in war. Either way they are not consumed productively: they play no part in the production of future surplus value. Finally, raising the organic composition of capital in the arms manufacturing industries will cut the profit rate in this sector, which will slightly reduce the general rate of profit. But we know that capital will then be reallocated across the system—flowing from the arms sector into other, productive, sectors with a lower organic composition. Prices of production will increase in the arms industries and fall in other sectors as a result. This will cheapen constant and variable capital, again slowing the decline of the general rate of profit. In principle, any "luxury" spending can play this role. In practice, the military competition of the Cold War provided the terrain on which arms spending could stabilise the system.

However, the "permanent arms economy", as Kidron called it, contained the seeds of its own demise. First, while the tendency for the rate of profit to fall was slowed, it was not stopped altogether. By the mid-1970s it had fallen considerably. Second, certain economies were spared the burden of arms spending, notably Japan and Germany whose military budgets were restricted after the Second World War. The arms spending of the biggest powers stabilised the system as a whole, but Japanese and German productive investment could run ahead of US and Soviet investment. This ultimately increased pressure on profit rates in these economies but it also cut the prices of their output. Japanese and German manufacturers could, therefore, compete far more effectively on world markets through their exports and generate excess profits in these areas. The rise of these and other non-militarised state capitalisms led to a smaller share of the world economy being devoted to arms expenditure.

Meanwhile the US and the Soviet Union struggled with the immense costs of their weapons spending. The vast burden of the US's unsuccessful war against Vietnam was matched by the Soviet Union in Afghanistan. Arms spending today can still help stimulate an economy by providing employment and boosting demand. But it does not have the sustained stabilising effect it once had, and indeed it is a burden on the states that undertake such spending—unless they can find a way of using their weapons to strengthen their economic position.

Alongside the expansion of Japan and Germany during the post-war boom, and the increased pressure on the Cold War superpowers, came the rise of a whole series of smaller industrialising nations. In the period after the Second World War most former colonies won their independence and many set about building their own industrial base—typically using some variety of state capitalism. While there is nothing automatic about new capitalist powers being able to break through, it is not true to say that they can never do so. Some of the larger states, Brazil, Indian and China, for example, built up significant industrial bases. Some, such as Taiwan, South Korea and Malaysia, emulated the Japanese technique of state-led, export-orientated growth. While many of these economies have suffered periodic setbacks, the overall picture of capitalism changed in the post-war period. Alongside the great powers that dominated the world economy there were now a series of "sub-imperialist" powers that sought to play on a local level the role that the US and Soviet Union could play on a global level.

The return of crisis

THE gradual fall in the rate of profit in the 1950s and 1960s led to a succession of deep economic crises from the 1970s. The Keynesian methods that had become the "common sense" in the preceding period proved utterly incapable of solving what now seemed like intractable problems. Eventually most politicians, of whatever political stripe, ditched the Keynesian ideology in favour of some version of the older economic ideas. Monetarism and neoliberalism were now the order of the day. However, the change in ideology did not alter the continued role of the state, or the hierarchy of competing states shaping the world system. According to the Argentinian Marxist Atilio Boron, writing in 2005:

> Ninety six percent of [the biggest] 200 global and transnational companies have their headquarters in only eight countries, are legally registered as incorporated companies of eight countries; and their boards of directors sit in eight countries of metropolitan capitalism. Less than 2 percent of their boards of directors members are non-nationals, while more than 85 percent of all their technological developments have originated within their "national frontiers". Their reach is global, but their property and their owners have a clear national base.

And state budgets still made up a massive chunk of most countries' economies. Indeed, they grew in countries such as the US and Britain, despite rhetoric to the contrary. States still waged war on behalf of their capitalists and still stepped in to bail out failing companies when crisis threatened the system. The rhetoric of free trade has often been most important in attacking workers or imposing goods and services from powerful states on the weaker ones.

The world at the end of the long boom was certainly more globalised than it was at the start. Trade returned to and then exceeded its level in the 1920s, flows of finance became global as never before, and production was also increasingly organised across borders. These developments put pressure on states such as the Soviet Union, which had limited access to world markets and the global division of labour, and which therefore struggled to accumulate sufficiently to keep up with its rivals. Eventually the struggle to keep pace with the US broke the Soviet Union's economy. The uprisings that subsequently broke out in both the Soviet Union and its allies in Eastern Europe ended with the old "state capitalist" regimes being overthrown and replaced with systems closer to Western-style capitalism.

The end of the Cold War, which had fixed imperialism into a system of two competing camps, created the possibility of new imperialist rivalries emerging. Some countries had by now built up sufficient industrial bases, often using state capitalist methods, to begin to compete on a world scale. For instance, China experienced growth rates of about 10 percent a year for much of the 1990s and 2000s. Others had been sucked into the world of capitalism and then thrown back, lacking the resources and muscle to compete. Such has been the fate of many African countries.

Increased globalisation did not alter the unevenness of the world economy. Some areas remained far more "important" (from a capitalist perspective) than others.

Of course, capitalists are happy to exploit workers wherever it is most convenient and profitable. The attraction of many Third World economies for multinationals and the companies that supply them is that they provide vast pools of cheap labour. But it is not true that industry can simply "up and move" to the Third World. Capitalists still tend to invest where investment has already taken place. Here there are bigger and more lucrative markets, infrastructures based on decades of state and private investment, trained and healthy workforces, and networks of suppliers. Capitalism remains centred on Western Europe, North America, Japan, plus regions of China and a few newly industrialised countries such as South Korea.

Comparing the GDP of particular countries or regions with total world GDP can indicate the relative importance of different parts of the world system. In 1969 the US, Europe and Japan together accounted for about 80 percent of world GDP. By 2007, after 38 years of "globalisation", they still accounted for 70 percent of world GDP. Of this 10 percent slide, over half was made up by the growth of China. The size of the Latin American, African and Middle Eastern economies, relative to the system as a whole, had changed very little.

Patterns of trade also reflect the importance of different areas of the world and the extent of globalisation. To take the biggest economy in the world, total US imports in the mid-2000s were the equivalent of about 18 percent of its GDP—although its net imports (imports minus exports) were just 5 percent of GDP. Trade had grown, tripling over the preceding 15 years. But two thirds of the US's imports still came from the EU and Japan, Canada (the US's northern neighbour), Mexico (the US's southern neighbour) or China. In fact these countries represented a growing share of US imports. By far the biggest change was the growth of Chinese imports, but these represented the equivalent of just 2 percent of US GDP in 2005. They were more important to China, making up about 10 percent of Chinese GDP. They were also of great importance to the wider East Asian economy. Some 70 percent of US imports from China contained components or materials from other economies in the region. If by globalisation we mean that more production is organised across national boundaries and some significant new centres of capital accumulation have emerged, then globalisation is a reality. If, however, globalisation is held to be a tendency towards the abolition of uneven development and the nation-state's role as an economic actor, then this has certainly not happened.

It is also a myth that globalisation and the rise of multinationals make it impossible for workers to fight. Multinationals do rely increasingly on a global division of labour and "just in time" production methods. But this can give workers in one part of the world tremendous power. For example, when 3,500 US workers who make vehicle axles took strike action in February 2008 their action rapidly closed down a whole series of General Motors plants they supplied. Another strike in 2008, by Boeing machinists, concentrated in one of the company's factories, cost the multinational over $100 million a day. The strike's impact was felt among suppliers as far away as Japan (Fuji Heavy Industries) and France (Safran), as well as in other US companies.

If myths abound about globalisation, this is even more the case when it comes to the nature of the modern working class. Some countries have seen a decline in certain industrial jobs. During the ten years from 1997 about 1.5 million manufacturing jobs were lost in Britain—causing great hardship for these workers. In the same period a similar number of financial sector jobs were created. Some were highly paid positions but the bulk were routine menial jobs in call centres or sitting at a computer processing data. While this may not look like a traditional factory, the drudgery, pay and conditions, and management bullying are the same. In general, the surprising thing about the world of work is not how much it has changed but how little. The same process of exploitation and accumulation, identified by Marx 150 years ago, is still central to the dynamic of capitalism. Exploitation is still centred on the workplace, where managers can bully and cajole workers, and bring them together with accumulations of dead labour.

The question of whether workers are producing goods or services is of little relevance. The worker who assembles a computer in Indonesia can, in general, identify something in common with a worker who assembles a Big Mac hamburger in Britain. Their lives appear a world apart, yet the common experience of alienation and exploitation lays the basis for solidarity between them.

In some ways the conditions faced by workers in recent years have become worse. Ruling classes the world over responded to the return of crisis in the 1970s by restructuring and increasing exploitation to drive up profit rates. This assault was begun very effectively in Britain under Margaret Thatcher and in the US under Ronald Reagan. Breaking powerful groups of unionised workers and encouraging bosses to go on the offensive helped to increase the share of wealth going to the ruling class, and their attempts were echoed elsewhere. This, and a clearout of some unprofitable units of capital, boosted profit rates from the late 1980s, though not to their level in the 1960s or the 1950s.

The partial restoration of profit rates did not restore the system to good health. For instance, the US suffered recessions in 1973-5, 1980-2, 1990-1 and 2001-3. The attempts to drive up profit rates also created new problems. If wages are held down, or even cut, how does the capitalist system ensure that all of its output is purchased and consumed, avoiding the problem of overproduction? If profit rates were very high capitalists could simply purchase the outputs of other capitalists. There may be little rationality to such a process of endless accumulation but it makes sense in capitalist terms. When the profit rate is not high enough to sustain such high levels of accumulation the output of capitalism must be consumed in other ways. From the 1990s through to the middle of this decade levels of personal debt increased at enormous speed as workers consumed more while being paid the same or even less. So in the ten years up to 2007 personal debt in the US grew from about 2.5 times the country's GDP to about 3.5 times. The equivalent of an entire year's economic output was accumulated as debt over that period. Such an expansion of debt can only continue up to a point, the point at which workers panic about their indebtedness and their future prospects, and those lending to them panic about getting their cash back.

A second factor also disguised underlying economic problems. Once accumulation slows, those capitalists with money to spend cannot find obvious outlets in the productive economy. Instead they look to the financial system and markets in fictitious capital to generate profits. This can mean lending to governments or banks, or it can mean speculating on assets prices such as those of shares or property. It can mean gambling on increasingly sophisticated financial instruments and other bets. For a while this can give the appearance of growth and prosperity. But eventually bubbles deflate or, more likely, suddenly burst.

The problem faced by capitalism today is a product of the two long-term trends discussed in this work. As the system ages it requires economic crisis—a clearing out of the system—to restore profit rates. But because units of capital get bigger over time, through the processes of centralisation and concentration of capital, such a crisis presents an ever greater risk to the system.

The constant temptation is to look for ways to generate profits outside the "real", value producing, economy and to look for mechanisms that spread the cost of crisis across the system as a whole rather than letting large chunks of the system go under. Another long-term trend, the growth of "waste" in the system— huge areas of unproductive expenditure—can slow down the tendency towards crisis by curtailing the rate of investment, but it also reduces the dynamism of the system.

Capitalism is far from stagnant. Booms can take off in certain areas of the system for certain periods of time. But these booms often threaten to destabilise the wider system. So the growth of China in the 1990s and the early to mid-2000s introduced huge imbalances into the system. China sold goods to US consumers and simultaneously lent money to America, for instance by building up huge quantities of US Treasury bonds. Such a virtuous circle can rapidly go into reverse, turning into a vicious circle helping to drag down both economies, as began to happen in 2008.

And booms associated with rapid accumulation can all too easily slip back. The 1980s saw an endless output of literature claiming that Japan would overtake the US and become the world's greatest economy. But by the 1990s the Japanese economy had fallen into economic stagnation, from which it had still not recovered at the time of writing.

It is difficult to see a return to the generalised boom and high profit rates of the post-war golden age unless there is an extremely destructive "clearing out" of capital. A sharp and severe economic crisis is one possibility. Another is war. The drive to war has become stronger in recent years. The US emerged from the Second World War with 50 percent of world production contained within its borders. Today the figure is just 25 percent. Yet the US still contributes just short of 50 percent of world arms spending. This creates circumstances in which the temptation for the US ruling class to use its military might to compensate for its economic decline is enormous. George Bush seized on the 11 September 2001 attacks on the US to do just this. Such a policy is risky—as seen by the disastrous invasions and occupations of Afghanistan and Iraq in 2001 and 2003. But the barbarity of capitalism permits our rulers to gamble with far more than money.

The drive to war is intensified by the changes in the balance of economic power in the world, with the rise of new economic powers such as China, which will want to play the game of global imperialist conflict on an even footing with other powers. Any economic crisis threatens to raise the tension between rival ruling classes as they struggle to shift the burden of the crisis onto each other and struggle to grab what surplus value they can.

Finally, the ecological destructiveness of capitalism as it drives to accumulate, in particular the way that carbon-based fuels have become its lifeblood, poses new problems. Global warming will hit workers and the global poor hardest, leading to struggles over food supplies and clean water, for example. It will also be another potential factor in the struggles between rival states and groups of capitalists.

If the tensions between capitalists can lead to horror, they can also create the conditions in which workers step forward and attempt to impose their solutions. Cracks at the top of the system can lead to ideological uncertainty and splits among our rulers. Simultaneously, the tensions between capitalists and workers can threaten to spill over into open conflict. There is nothing inevitable about workers' revolt. It is a political question, and it requires, among other things, an organised political response from those who are convinced of the need for a socialist alternative to capitalism in order for them to win over those who are not yet convinced. But while socialism is far from inevitable, the constant tussle between capital and labour—sometimes hidden, sometimes open, as Marx put it—will continue for as long as capitalism continues. In that conflict lie the seeds of something very different: a world structured according to the needs of its population, rather than the drive for profit; run democratically from below, rather than from on high by capitalists and their supporters; a world of socialism rather than a world of barbarism.

Appendix 1

Marx's theory of rent

Marx's theory of rent shows how capitalist accumulation proceeds in the presence of landowners capable of capturing some of the surplus value squeezed out of workers. Here I will merely provide a brief, and somewhat simplified, summary of Marx's account. (This appendix assumes that the reader is familiar with the concept of prices of production and costs of production outlined in the chapter "Prices and the General Rate of Profit".)

Marx begins with a simple illustration of the concept of rent. He considers what would happen if a capitalist built a factory on land with a waterfall capable of driving a waterwheel and providing power. Assuming that this could achieve everything that rival capitalists achieved with steam power, the capitalist with the waterfall would have an advantage. If the price of production of the output of the factory was £120 and the cost of production using steam power was £100, the profit received by the capitalists using steam power would be £20. If the cost of production for the capitalist using a waterwheel was just £80, they would instead receive £40 in profit. It is not that the waterfall creates any new surplus value. The point is that access to this natural phenomenon reduces costs of production relative to those of other capitalists. Up to this point it is assumed that the capitalist with the waterfall gains all of the excess profit. But Marx then writes:

Now let us assume that the waterfalls, along with the land to which they belong, are held by individuals who are regarded as owners of these portions of the earth, ie who are landowners. These owners prevent the investment of capital in the waterfalls and their exploitation by capital. They can permit or forbid such utilisation. But a waterfall cannot be created by capital out of itself. Therefore, the surplus profit which arises from the employment of this waterfall is not due to capital, but to the utilisation of a natural force which can be monopolised, and has been monopolised, by capital. Under these circumstances, the surplus profit is transformed into ground-rent, that is, it falls into the possession of the owner of the waterfall.

He then seeks to apply to agriculture this general concept, in which landowners capture excess profits by controlling capital's access to land. He also suggests that a similar method could be used more generally, for instance by applying it to mining and building sites.

Marx analyses agricultural rents through three different categories. The first he calls "differential rent I". This is rent that arises when "equal quantities of capital and labour are applied on equal areas of land with unequal results". This might be due to the natural fertility of the soil or due to an exceptionally good location of the land, although Marx focuses on the former. Here some or all of the excess profits generated by capitalist farmers with access to land of greater fertility can be captured by landowners—provided they are sufficiently powerful to do so.

"Differential rent II" considers the impact of changing the amount of capital invested on different plots of land, or indeed on the same plot of land in successive periods.

If the yield produced simply doubled each time invest-ment doubled the situation would be unchanged. But what if, say, the doubling of investment doubled the yield of low quality land, while quadrupling the yield of the best quality land; or if the first doubling of invest-ment on a particular plot quadrupled the yield but a subsequent doubling of investment only doubled the yield? Differential rent II analyses the additional rent that might be captured by landowners in such situations.

Marx stresses that differential rent II cannot be un-derstood in the absence of differential rent I, because different capitals are always applied in the context of uneven qualities of land in differing locations. And in-deed, the question of what constitutes good or bad land is shaped historically by the availability of different farming techniques and scientific methods. The two forms of differential rent cannot simply be added to-gether. They must instead be studied in their various historically fashioned combinations. Marx provides de-tailed examples of some possible combinations.

Finally, "absolute rent" is a consequence of differ-ences between the agriculture sector and other sectors of the economy. If agriculture had a lower organic compo-sition of capital we would expect capital to flow into this sector, lowering prices of production below the value of the output and, eventually, leading to an equal-isation of profit rates between the different sectors. But if this flow of capital is impeded, agricultural goods will be sold above their prices of production—and landown-ers can capture the difference as absolute rent, in addition to any differential rent.

As this brief account suggests, rent is one of the most concrete and complicated subjects dealt with in *Capital*. The reading list at the end of this book points to more de-tailed works that cover this topic. Ben Fine and Alfredo

Saad-Filho's *Marx's Capital* gives an excellent and succinct summary of Marx's theory. David Harvey's ambitious book *Limits to Capital*, along with his later works, seeks to generalise Marx's theory of rent to construct an elaborate theory of the spatial organisation and development of capitalism, and to understand how this modifies patterns of economic crisis.

Appendix 2

The "transformation problem"

Marx's account of the transformation of values into prices of production, which I described in the chapter "Prices and the General Rate of Profit", has proved remarkably controversial, spawning the debate surrounding what is known as the "transformation problem". The various positions on this debate are too numerous and complex to summarise in an introductory work such as this. Instead I shall briefly, and as simply as possible, summarise two promising approaches and criticise one poor approach.

The controversy springs from the question of the "transformation of input values". In the examples he gives in the third volume of *Capital* Marx shows how commodities that are produced with certain values end up with certain prices of production. But it appears as if the inputs into production are purchased by the capitalist at their values rather than their prices of production. Marx comments in *Capital*:

> We had originally assumed that the cost price of a commodity [ie the cost to the capitalist of producing it] equalled the value of the commodities consumed in its production. But for the buyer the price of production of a specific commodity is its cost price, and may thus pass as cost price into the prices of other commodities. Since the price of production may differ from the value of a commodity, it follows that the cost price of a commodity containing this price of production of another

commodity may also stand above or below that portion of its total value derived from the value of the means of production consumed by it.

One interpretation of this passage is to say that the inputs must also be transformed, a complicated mathematical procedure. According to this interpretation, the fundamental role of Marx's transformation is to show that prices of production are a complex form of value. Marx was not particularly interested in a detailed theory for calculating the prices of commodities; he was more interested in showing how prices emerge and how surplus value is redistributed through the system. However, once the new step of transforming the inputs is taken, there are essentially two separate systems—prices and values—one measuring the passage of labour time through the system, one measuring the amounts of money exchanged to purchase commodities at various stages.

A second family of interpretations, known as "single-system" interpretations, began to emerge in different forms in the 1980s. According to these interpretations prices of production are the amount of *value* that the capitalist must advance in order to purchase inputs. Prices of production are simply the way that values express themselves once the different sectors of the economy are taken into account. So prices can still be measured in either money or labour time, just as values were in the first volume of *Capital*. Many of the more advanced works in the suggested reading at the end of this book set out different solutions to the "transformation problem".

One unhelpful but influential way of solving the problem is the tradition founded by Ladislaus Bortkiewicz and others at the start of the 20th century. This began with the approach similar to the first interpretation I have described above. But Bortkiewicz went further by establishing a series of "simultaneous equations" linking together the inputs and outputs of production for the economy. There is a huge problem with such an approach. It assumes that in any given cycle of production the price of a commodity at the beginning, when used as an input, is the same as at the end when it emerges as an output. So if we take a year as our cycle of production, in Borkiewicz's system the price of a printing press bought by a capitalist on 1 January 2009 would be identical to the price of the same printing press produced by the manufacturer on 31 December 2009, 364 days later. But one of the central features of Marx's economics is that the economy is *not* in equilibrium. Prices change; capitalists accumulate and compete. In order to calculate the price of an input into a cycle of production it is essential to look at the price it has when it leaves the *previous* cycle of production. Ignoring this straightforward point may allow complex systems of equations to be constructed, but it destroys the essence of Marx's theory.

Further reading

Online

The Marxist Internet Archive (www.marxists.org) contains many of the works by Marx and Engels quoted in this book, including full versions of the three volumes of *Capital*, the *Grundrisse* and the *Contribution to the Critique of Political Economy*.

Recent issues of *International Socialism* journal are now available online (www.isj.org.uk). Among its contents are many articles on Marxist political economy and its application to contemporary capitalism.

Some of the earlier articles from this journal are available from the Marxist Internet Archive or the *Socialist Review* and *International Socialism* Index (www.socialistreviewindex.org.uk). ResistanceMP3 (www.resistanceMP3.org.uk) contains a wealth of audio recordings on Marxist political economy and other subjects.

Many of the writings of the economist Anwar Sheikh are available online (http://homepage.newschool.edu/~AShaikh/). The essay "An Introduction to the History of Crisis Theories" influenced the presentation of the chapter on crisis here. "Explaining Inflation and Unemployment" gives an interesting Marxist take on inflation.

Marx and Marxism

Alex Callinicos's *The Revolutionary Ideas of Karl Marx* (Bookmarks) is, by a considerable margin, the best guide to the full range of Marx's theory.

Revolution in the 21st Century by Chris Harman (Bookmarks) is recommended for those wanting to get to grips with the tradition of "socialism from below" that Marx and Engels founded.

Various editions of Marx's *Capital* are available. The traditional hardback volumes, often mass produced versions of the original translation by Samuel Moore and Edward Aveling from 1887, are easily obtained from secondhand bookshops. A different translation by Ben Fowkes was produced by Penguin in 1976 and is also widely available. The Fowkes version aims to translate more accurately certain terms that Marx used. However, the Moore and Aveling version is probably more readable and closer to the spirit of Marx's mission to make *Capital* accessible to working class readers.

The best introductions to Marx and Engels's ideas in their own words include the *Communist Manifesto*; *Socialism: Utopian and Scientific*; *Wages, Prices and Profits*; and *The Civil War in France*. Various selections of Marx and Engels's works are available. Here the modern versions do improve on traditional selections by giving greater weight to Marx's early writings—vital for an understanding of alienation. Two good collections are David McLellan's *Karl Marx: Selected Writings* (Oxford University) and Robert Tucker's *Marx-Engels Reader* (Norton).

For those wishing to get to grips with Marx's early writings, István Mészáros's book *Marx's Theory of Alienation* (Merlin), though a difficult read, is unsurpassed as a guide.

Introductory texts on Marxist political economy

Chris Harman's *Economics of the Madhouse* (Bookmarks) gave many of us our first introduction to Marx's understanding of capitalism and is easily the most accessible work on this subject.

Marx's Capital by Ben Fine and Alfredo Saad-Filho (Pluto) is an excellent guide to Marx's writing. Aimed primarily at students, it covers material that parallels that in this work.

Isaac Rubin's *History of Economic Thought* (Pluto) is the best guide to the development of classical economic theory by a Marxist writer and helps give context to Marx's writings.

Anti-Capitalism: A Marxist Introduction, edited by Alfredo Saad-Filho (Pluto), contains a collection of essays by leading Marxist academics covering a range of topics related to political economy.

More advanced texts on Marxist economics

David Harvey's *Limits to Capital* (Verso) is a monumental work. The author does not simply present Marx's ideas but also engages carefully with them, and Harvey's own work deserves to be treated similarly. The sections on finance and fictitious capital here draw heavily on Harvey's presentation. Harvey also discusses Marx's concept of rent in detail, giving it a central role in understanding the geography of capitalism.

Rereading Capital by Ben Fine and Lawrence Harris (Macmillan) is a very good account of Marx's theory published 1979, although marked by a certain style of academic Marxism popular at the time. The account of the organic composition and value composition of capital given here derives from Fine and Harris's work.

Isaac Rubin's *Essays on Marx's Theory of Value* (Black Rose) is a difficult, but ultimately rewarding, work on the concept of value that underpins Marxist economic theory.

Chris Harman's *Explaining the Crisis* (Bookmarks) applies Marx's analysis to capitalism as it develops and explores the nature of economic crises. The final section of this book draws heavily on Harman's writing.

A new work by Chris Harman, due out in 2009, will give a comprehensive account of the development of capitalism in the 20th century and its shape today—something only outlined briefly here.

Frontiers of Political Economy by Guglielmo Carchedi (Verso), though hard to get hold of, is a brilliant work. In it Carchedi attempts to apply Marxist economics to contemporary capitalism, looking at inflation, the interaction of different national economies and the relationship between production and circulation.

Capital and Theory by Mike Kidron (Pluto) is an important collection of essays, some of which are now available online from the Marxist Internet Archive. Kidron's ideas on arms spending as a factor providing temporary stability to capitalism after the Second World War were crucial in explaining capitalism's "golden age".

Andrew Kliman's recent book *Reclaiming Marx's Capital* (Lexington) sets out the "temporal single system interpretation" of *Capital*, which I mention here in the context of the "transformation problem". Kliman's criticisms of accounts that see capitalism as a static system in equilibrium are well made and the work as a whole is very readable.

Alfredo Saad-Filho's *Value of Marx* (Routledge) is a difficult (and expensive) work. But it engages with some of the important debates surrounding Marx's "value theory" and puts forward another approach to the "transformation problem".

The Law of Accumulation and the Breakdown of the Capitalist System by Henryk Grossmann (Pluto) is another classic work, which sought to show how the crisis of capitalism originates in the process of accumulation itself.

The two volumes by Michael Howard and John King under the title *A History of Marxian Economics* (Macmillan) provide a comprehensive history of Marxist political economy since Marx.